N ssics

Franke

HOVE FOTO BOOKS

NIKON MODERN CLASSICS

Printed in Guernsey
in the British Channel Islands

by

The Guernsey Press Company Limited
Commercial Printing Division
P.O Box 57
Braye Road, Vale
Guernsey, Channel Islands,
G.B. Europe

Tel No. (01481) 45866 Fax No. (01481) 49907

Guernsey Press, Specialist Printers of Paperback Books,
Newspapers and high quality full colour literature

COMPLETE Nikon USER'S GUIDE

MODERN CLASSICS

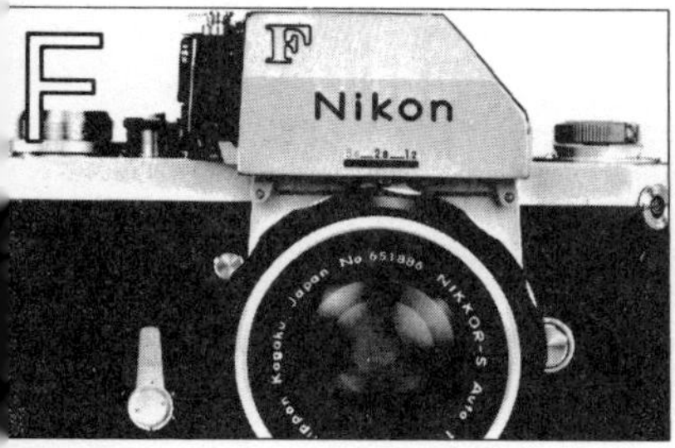

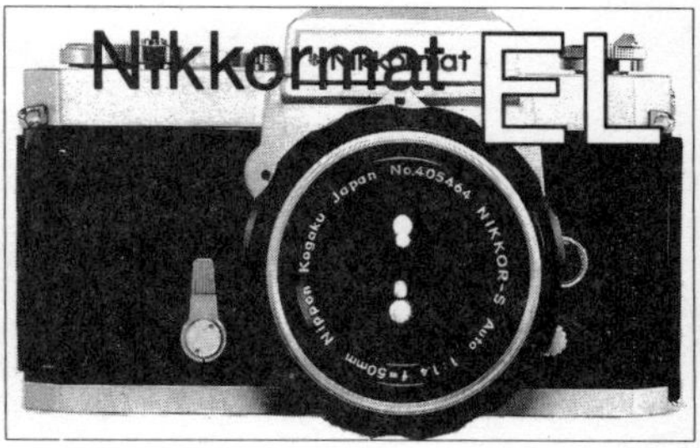

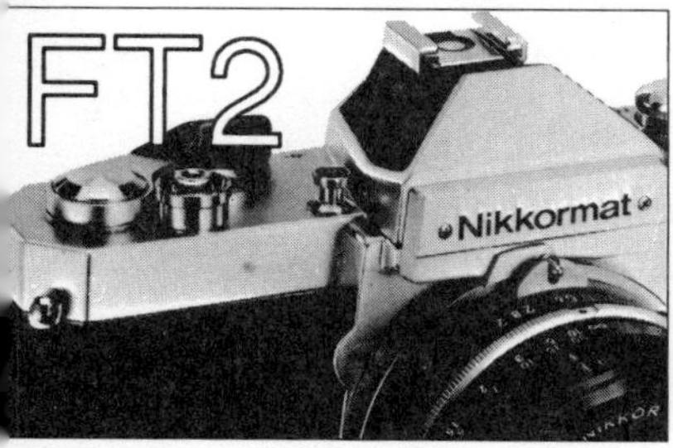

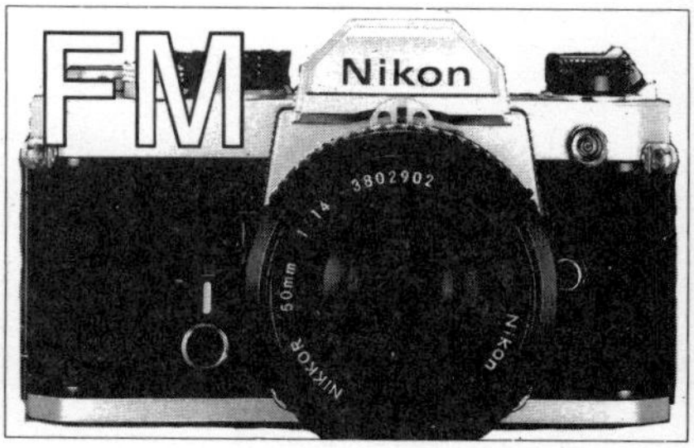

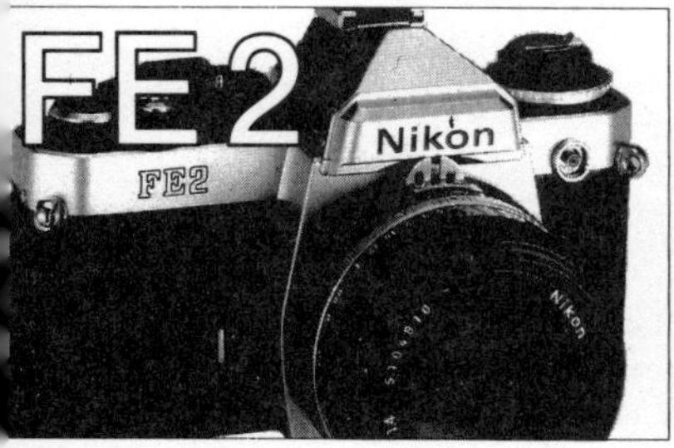

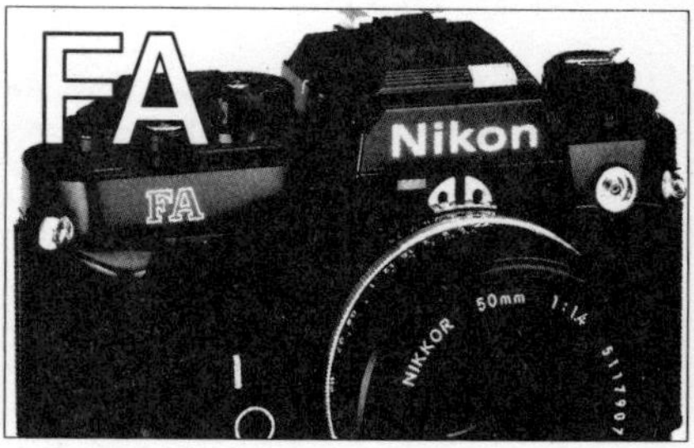

AN ORIGINAL
HOVE FOTO BOOKS

Harald Francke

Nikon Modern Classics

First English Edition April 1991
Published by Hove Foto Books
Reprinted January 1993
Reprinted May 1996

Published by Hove Foto Books
Hotel de France, St Saviour's Road
St Helier, Jersey, Channel Islands JE2 7LA

Printed by
The Guernsey Press Co Ltd, Commercial Printing Division
Guernsey, Channel Islands

British Library Cataloguing in Publication Data
Francke, Harald
Users guide to Nikon modern classics.
1. Cameras
I. Title II. Nikon-kameras von Gestern fur
Anwender von Heute. English 771.31

ISBN 0-906447-75-95

Worldwide Distribution
Newpro (UK) Ltd
Old Sawmills Road
Faringdon, Oxon
SN7 7DS, England
Tel: (01367) 242411 Fax: (01367) 241124

Contents

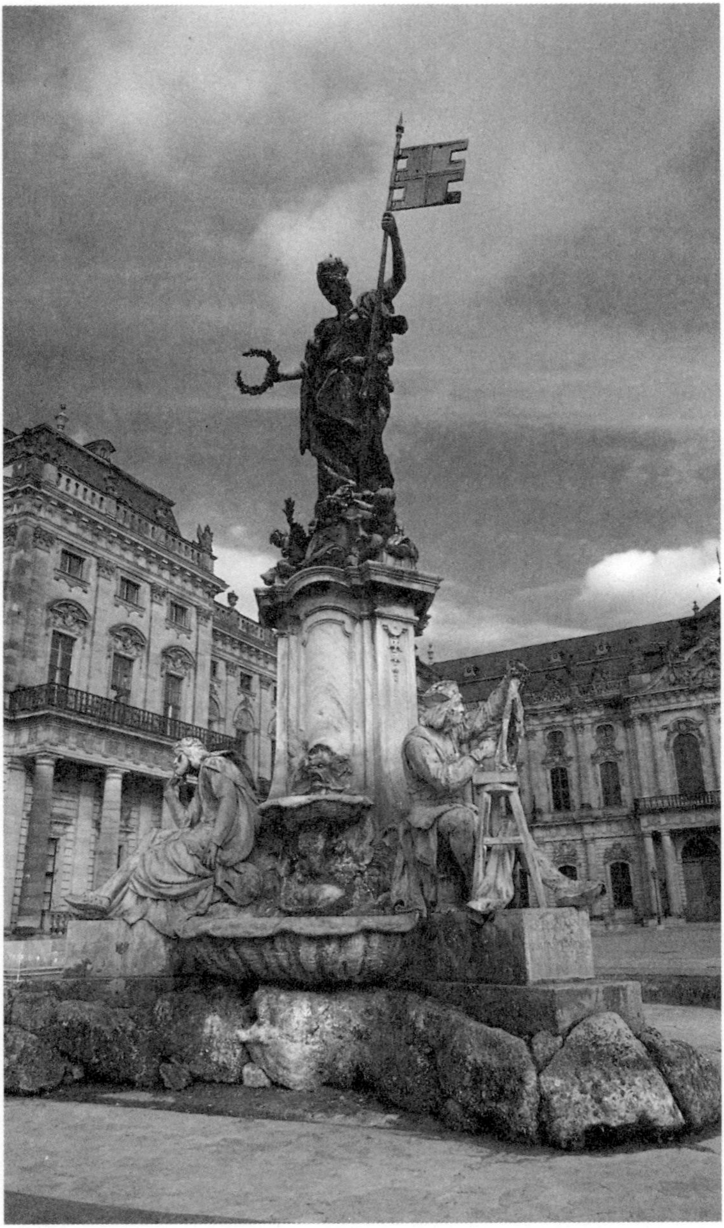

Cameras of Yesterday

The cameras introduced in this book are not only from yesterday but also from the day before! Bearing in mind that photographic technology is advancing with great speed these cameras should perhaps be thrown on the scrap heap or at best grace the shelves of collectors' homes.

But this is not really the point at all.

Naturally photographic technology has developed a great deal since 1983 when the Nikon FE2 and FA, the youngest of the cameras dealt with in this book, came on the market. Autofocus is now a matter of course for SLR cameras; they feature motor drives to advance the film, multiple exposure is now incorporated into automatic TTL flashes and tiny TTL flash units are built into the viewfinder housings to enable a camera to be used wherever and whenever. However, the light still enters the camera from the lens, and the focal plane shutter still opens and closes to enable the light to reach the film. The aperture can still be used to control the depth of field, the shutter's fast and slow speeds can still freeze movement or render it blurred, and, most importantly, the photographer still needs to hold the camera to his eye in order to assess the subject in the viewfinder, to determine the framing of the view and to press the shutter release at the right moment.

They're not as old as the fountain in this photograph, and they don't have their own monument like Walther von der Vogelweide, who is shown on the left with his legs crossed, but the old Nikons are always worth considering when you are buying a camera.

If the photographer is unable to do all these, even the most sophisticated camera is useless. If the photographer can visualize his picture before he releases the shutter, however, then he can use any camera to transform his ideas into the right picture. So why not use one of the older Nikon cameras, which can be bought quite cheaply secondhand? These cameras were built solidly and feature everything needed for the composition of good pictures (the more modern versions feature even more). Even the Nikon cameras of the 60s, 70s and 80s are still integrated in the Nikon system and can be used with modern lenses and accessories.

But now about this book.

It is not intended for Nikon collectors who need to know about even the minutest technical modification during the development of a model; neither is it aimed at the Nikon photographer wanting to gain new knowledge about the camera they have been using for years.

This book is intended as a short introduction to the Nikon system and shows a selection from its range. It might help the undecided to go for a particular camera. It can help the buyer of one of these six cameras to find his way around it, because it is quite likely that the instruction manual has been lost. It can help the novice photographer assess the technical possibilities of these cameras as well as use them.

In the years since 1959 when the Nikon F was first introduced many lenses with a Nikon bayonet fitting have come on the market - plus a few variations which differ in a few important details.

You will find something about the bayonet variations in several places in this book and also in the chapter about lenses, but there is nothing about the different Nikon lenses themselves because a 35mm lens of 1959 achieves exactly the same as a 35mm lens of 1991.When a lens features a speed of f/2 the fact that it can be used hand-held longer than a f/4 with the same focal length applies to an old lens as much as to a new lens.

I hope that your entry into this interesting hobby is made easier and that the decision to choose one or the other older Nikon camera (or even several) is made simpler after reading this book.

Harald Francke

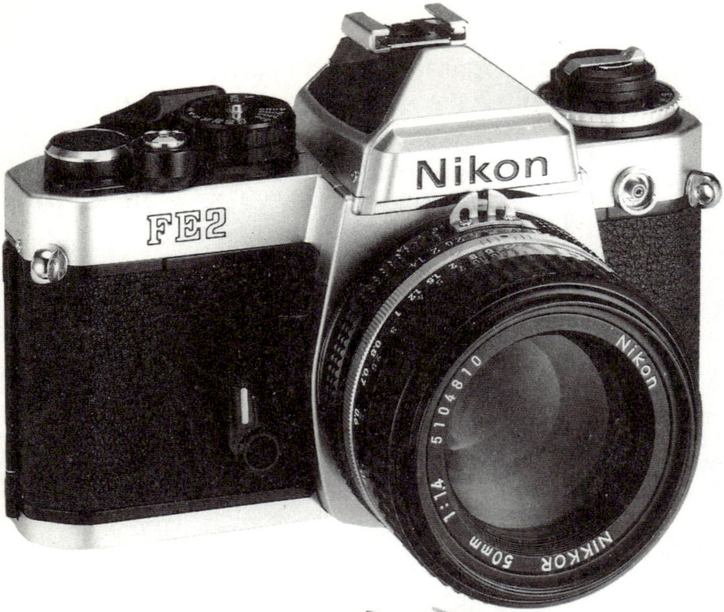
Nikon
FE2
NIKKOR 50mm 1:1.4 5104810
Nikon

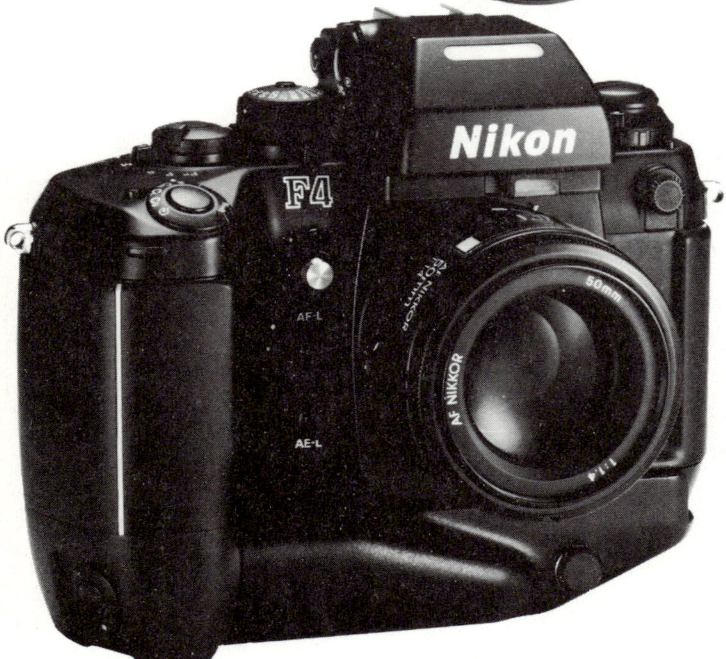
Nikon
F4
AF-L
AE-L
AF NIKKOR
50mm
1:1.4

Nikon - Then and Now

During the last few years there has been a change at Nikon. From a small manufacturer of professional cameras developed a producer who, although still providing fine professional cameras, is now aiming at the less ambitious photographer as well. The change is manifested in the quantities of cameras sold which brings Nikon into the league of the top five camera producers, where it has been for a long time, from the quality point of view. But the course to victory started a great deal earlier.

In 1917,when the battles of the First World War were still being fought, three large optical companies amalgamated in Japan and the name of the new company was Nippon Kogaku K.K.

Cameras were of minor importance in the first few years - other optical equipment such as spectacles, binoculars and telescopes were the mainstay of the company.

From there, however, it was only a small step towards camera lenses. These lenses, produced since 1931,were called Nikkors and under that name they could also be used with the cameras of other manufacturers. The Hansa-Canon of 1936 - mother of all Canon 35mm cameras - was on the market, for example, with an optional Nikkor 50mm,f/3.5 or Nikkor 50mm,f/4.5.

The Nikon 'oldies' and the modern autofocus SLR cameras are worlds apart in terms of both design and technology. But if you know how to make the most of the possibilities of the 'oldies' you will enjoy taking photographs with an FE-2 (or a Nikon F, or a Nikkormat EL, etc.) just as much as with the modern models.

The Second World War some three years later also involved Nippon Kogaku K.K.

Three years after the war the Nikon I, a 35mm rangefinder camera, came on the market. This, like all postwar Japanese cameras, was based on a German success. In this case not the Leica but its competitor, the Contax.

The range for the next 20 years consisted of such viewfinder cameras with a few variations, e.g., attachable motor drive..

The big step into the SLR market came in 1959 with the Nikon F, which offered all the features that characterized the professional camera - sturdiness and an ever-increasing modular system (interchangeable viewfinders, motor drives, lenses, bellows) that enabled the camera to be utilized in all kinds of situations a professional photographer might come across. The fact that the camera in extreme cases could end up as a rugged monster piece of equipment was irrelevant when taking into account all the possibilities.

A special feature is the viewfinder of the Nikon F - about 1962 an exposure metering viewfinder, the Photomic Head appeared equipped with an external sensor, followed by the Photomic T for internal metering in 1965.

The F2, which arrived in 1971 with the Nikon F and then replaced it, was also designed as a modular unit. While the body remained the same to a large extent, new viewfinders were added continuously, until aperture priority was also possible with this camera (the viewfinder in question was DP-12, supplemented by the control unit DS-12).

Running parallel with the professional cameras Nikon F and Nikon F2 in all their variations was the series of Nikkormat cameras aimed at the dedicated amateur. The viewfinders were not interchangeable nor was there - at least to begin with - a connection for a motor drive. The Nikkormat FS and FT from 1965, the

FTn from 1967, the FT2 from 1975 and finally the FT3 from 1977 - basically the same as the FT2 but featuring the new AI lens connection - were all part of that series.

A separate group within the Nikkormat range of cameras were the EL from 1972, the ELW from 1976 - the first Nikkormat with winder connection - and the EL2 from 1977, replacing the ELW and like the FT3 featuring the AI lens connection.

While six new SLR cameras appeared in 1977, only one of them was of real importance - the Nikon FM starting a new family within the Nikon system. This family included the FE from 1978, the FM2 from 1982 - the first camera in the world to feature a shutter speed of $^{1}/_{4000}$ sec - and the FE2 from 1983 with a fastest flash sync speed of $^{1}/_{250}$ sec.

Loosely related to these cameras was the FA from 1983 which caused a stir with its multiple exposure metering, but it was not realized at the time what a promising piece of technology that was for the future.

Another line of Nikon SLR cameras appeared simultaneously - the beginner cameras - with the EM appearing in 1979. This was a very popular camera, perhaps too popular for the tastes of the "professional amateur". But the success of this little one proved Nikon right and in 1982 it was followed by the FG and two years later by the FG-20. Whereas these three cameras were found at the bottom of the price scale, the new professional camera F3 was placed at the top. This appeared in 1980, featured an attachable motor drive, interchangeable viewfinder, and automatic exposure metering. A special viewfinder and two extra lenses turned the F3, in 1983, into an autofocus camera - two years ahead of the AF revolution led by the Minolta 7000.

In the same year the Nikon company really opened up the market of popular compact cameras for the 80s and 90s. Autofocus, automatic exposure metering, built-in motor and flash are features of the L35AF which was also available in a databack version. In the following years Nikon brought out a whole range of those small, carry-around cameras such as the Nikon TW20 which was supposed to avoid the red-eye effect with a special flash system - a technique that was to be incorporated into many other compact cameras.

1985 marked a change. The Nikon F-301 appeared with built-in motor and two automatic programs. The Nikon F-501 followed a year later, very similar to the F-301 but featuring autofocus. Nikon, although rather reticent towards new trends and ideas in the past, were quick in their decision in this instance and backed the right horse. The important thing is that the bayonet of the Nikon F from 1959 still forms the base for the lens connection, although it had been greatly improved over the years.

In 1987 the Nikon F-401 with built-in flash came on the market and two years later a new, modified version, the F-401s, appeared.

In 1988 Nikon introduced the F-801, a very comprehensively-equipped camera appealing to both amateur and professional alike. But although the F-801 was a top-of-the-range camera Nikon themselves topped it with another one in the same year. The new professional camera F4 (F4S with ultra fast motor) was quite a chunk of photographic machinery.

During the Photokina year of 1990 all those people preferring to do without autofocus were taken into account once more. The new F-601 is available as an AF or an M version - on the whole a superfluous decision as every Nikon AF SLR camera from the F-501 to the F4 can be used with manually focusing Nikkors.

The Nikonos I, an underwater camera with interchangeable viewfinders, appeared in 1963 and was still around in its latest version in 1984.

As proven at Photokina 1988 Nikon did not rest on the laurels gained with the cameras of the last 40 years but looked to the future. The Nikon QV 1000 C is a functional black-and-white stills video camera whose pictures can be transmitted across the world via the telephone line. Although this camera is no substitute for the F4 - and is not intended to be - it demonstrates what press photography could look like around the turn of the millennium.

Nikon F - How It All Started

The fact that "Nikon" is a synonym for "professional 35mm camera" is based on a camera of which it is said that you could hammer nails into the wall with it and still carry on shooting. This camera is the Nikon F which can be regarded as the mother of all Nikon SLR cameras. What are the features - apart from the legendary character - of the Nikon F?

When Nikon introduced the 35mm SLR Model "F" in 1959 many professional photographers were still convinced that a Leica rangefinder camera was the only adequate vehicle for 35mm films and that most other tasks were best tackled by a twin lens Rolleiflex. It needs to be mentioned, though, that the popular Leica M2 of the time did not have an exposure meter and the Rolleiflex could not accommodate interchangeable lenses.

The Nikon F is also not equipped with all the technical possibilities which make photography easier but not necessarily better today.

Basically the Nikon F is a very simple camera which by adding various attachments can be used in many photographic situations.

Exposure Metering - with Nikon accessories

The Nikon F has no exposure meter as a standard feature. But the prism finder can be exchanged for an exposure metering finder (model Photomic TN or Photomic FTN), and if such a finder is not available you can do without just as well.

The prism finder of the Nikon F can be removed from the camera by pressing the locking button - about a

The Photomic FTn finder turns the standard Nikon F into a great camera. The speed preselection scale is visible on the viewfinder. The old Nikkors are distinguished by a lengthy engraving around the bezel.

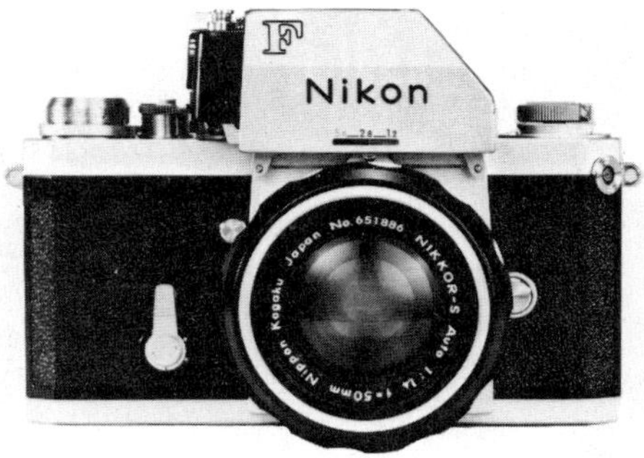

finger's breadth from the viewfinder - with a matchstick, point of a ballpoint or similar object and lifting off the prism. The metering prism can now simply be pushed onto the body and is locked into position.

The metering finder Photomic FTN operates on two CdS cells, which will not impress anyone today as the fast silicon cells are generally used now. But at the time of the Nikon F cadmium sulphide cells were a novelty as the majority of exposure meters depended on selenium cells.

Selenium produces energy from the incoming light and this energy is metered and used to determine the brightness of the subject and thus the correct exposure. This is a useful feature as selenium exposure meters work always and everywhere.

CdS cells alter their electrical resistance according to the light. Although rather slow compared to modern silicon cells they do react faster than selenium cells, even when it is getting dark.

The use of CdS cells in the Photomic FTN was therefore logical at the time. But in order to meter a change in the resistance these cells need to be supplied with a current, i.e. the Photomic FTN requires power. This is supplied by batteries which need space. The Nikon F itself requires no power and therefore was not designed to accommodate batteries. And so it is no surprise that the Photomic FTN is rather a large

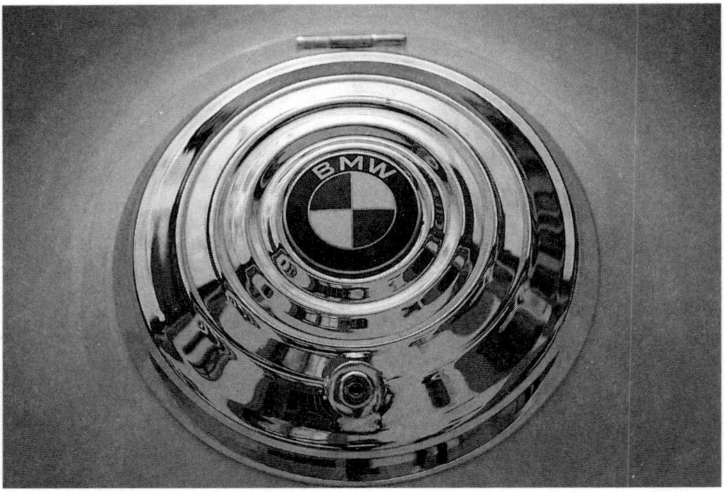

The strong central emphasis in this shot captured the bright centre of the subject and made the surrounding area a little too dark.

attachment as it has to house two button cells as well as the metering and indicating mechanisms.

The decision, to use the centre-weighted integrating exposure metering method was taken early on by Nikon but still effective today. This is a precise metering zone in the centre of the picture, clearly defined by a circle on the screen, which is weighted at 60% while the outer zone is weighted at 40%.

Two window subjects. Both shots get their appeal from the effect of looking through something at the subject: through the window at the nick-nacks on the window sill, then through the branches at the window. In the top shot the selected exposure was a little more generous to emphasise the playful mood; in the bottom shot a slight underexposure on the metered value was selected in order to turn the branch into a complete silhouette.

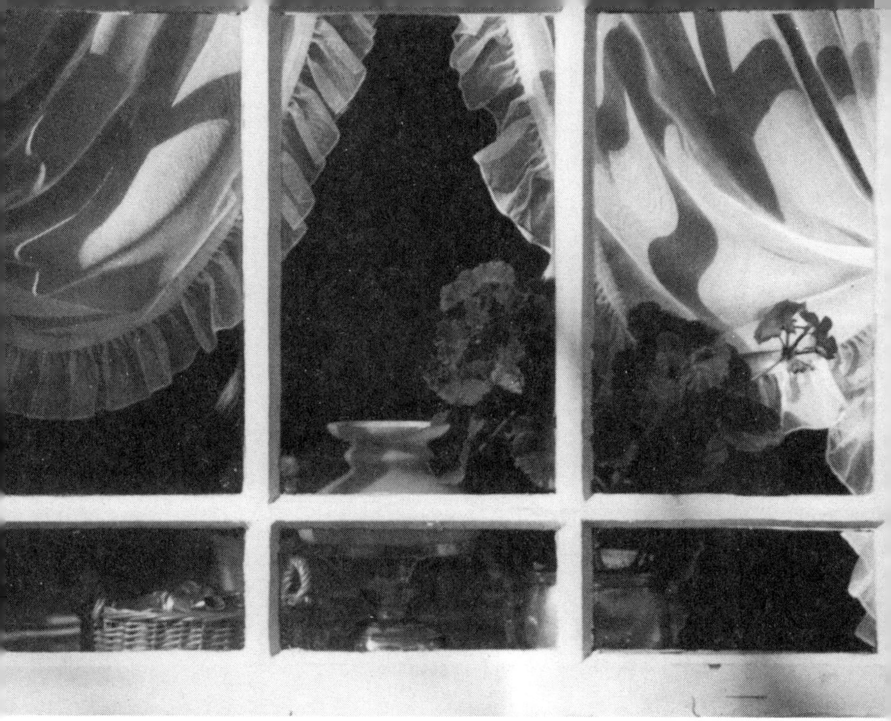

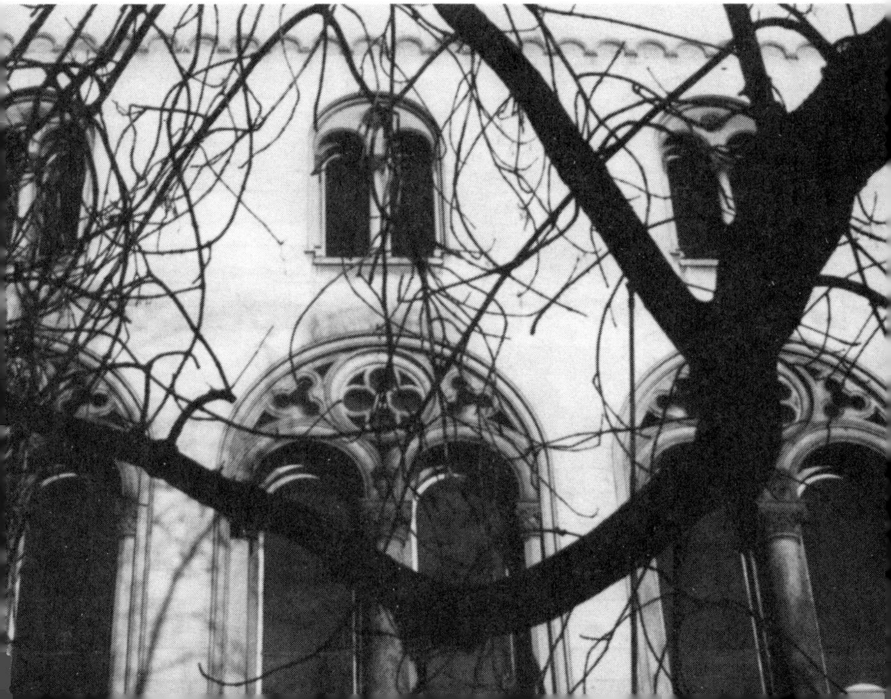

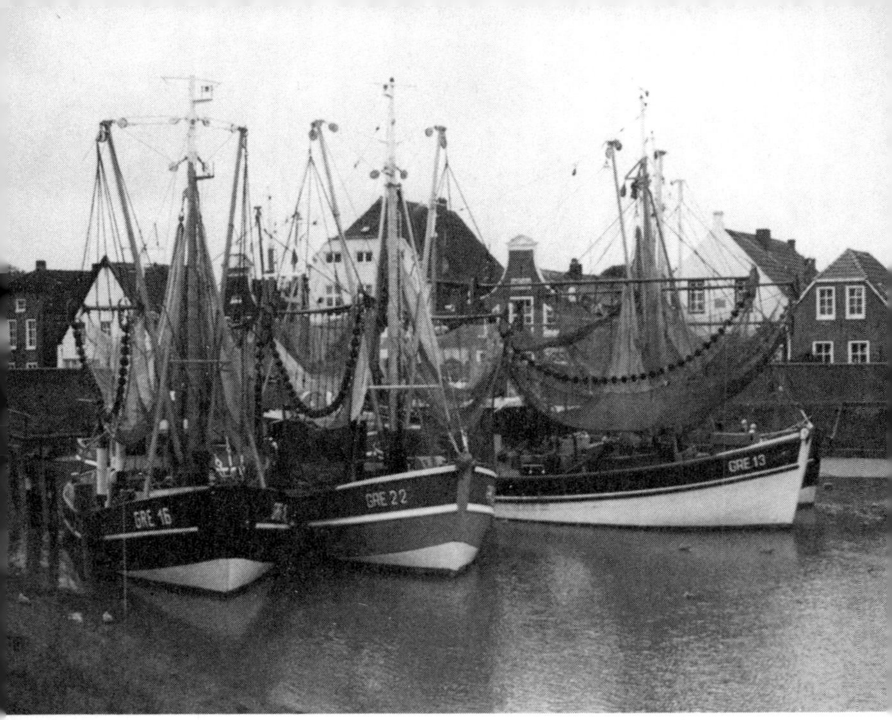
GRE 16
GRE 22
GRE 13

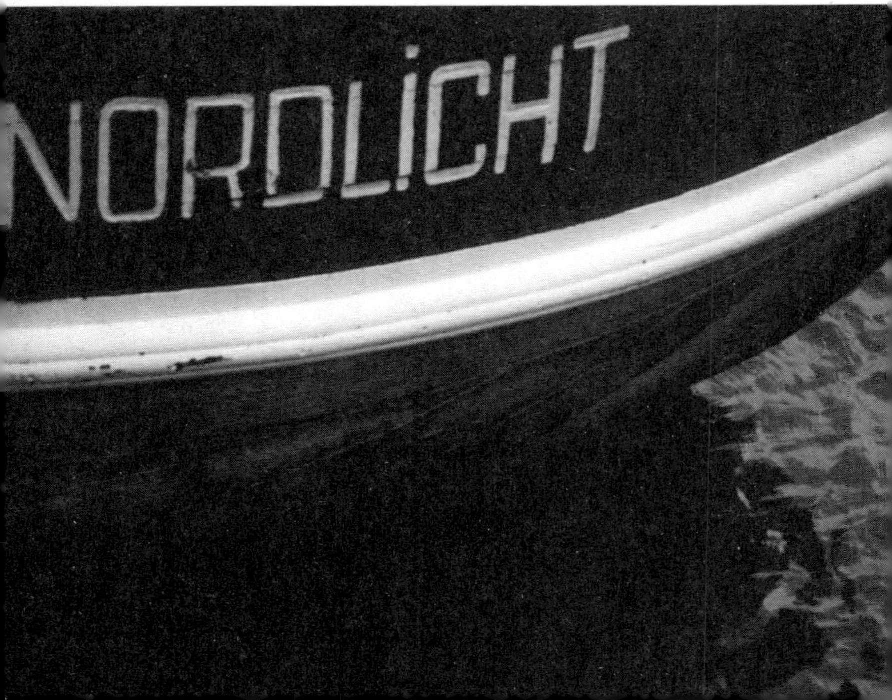
NORDLICHT

How does this division work? Each exposure meter, and the Photomic FTN is no exception, is set to an average grey value with an 18% reflection factor. As long as the subject basically corresponds to this average value in its light and shadow areas the picture will be exposed correctly. This is true for the majority of subjects, but obviously not for all. The separation of the metering area into an important and less important zone enables you to determine on which part of a subject differing from the given setting you want to base the exposure metering. You could leave very bright or very dark subject parts out if you wish, for example. With the Nikon F - and any suitably equipped later Nikon SLR camera - the metering angle can be determined very accurately for the given subject by close-up metering and the use of long focal lengths.

Another feature, apart from the division of the metering zone, relates this camera to the later Nikon SLRs. When exposure metering takes place through the lens with full aperture, the strength of the light and the aperture range of the lens must be transferred to the exposure meter and to this end the meter coupling prong on the aperture ring engages with a coupling pin on the lens mount of the camera. To work properly the aperture ring must be set to f/5.6.

A panorama shot like the photograph at the top belongs in the holiday album or slide show. But you shouldn't be content with just this shot. Details separated from the overall image with a telephoto lens intensify the mood.

Exposure Metering - with hand-held meters

What do you do when your Nikon F only has the normal prism finder or another finder without exposure meter?

Although today, over 30 years after the introduction of the Nikon F, almost all 35mm cameras are equipped with built-in exposure meters and automatic exposure features there are still hand-held exposure meters available.

At the bottom end of the price range is the exposure meter Hama Selen 1 which is a good choice when using your Nikon F without being dependent on batteries. It is compact with a metering range from EV2 to EV20 and the film speed can be set from ISO 6/9° to ISO 6400/39°.

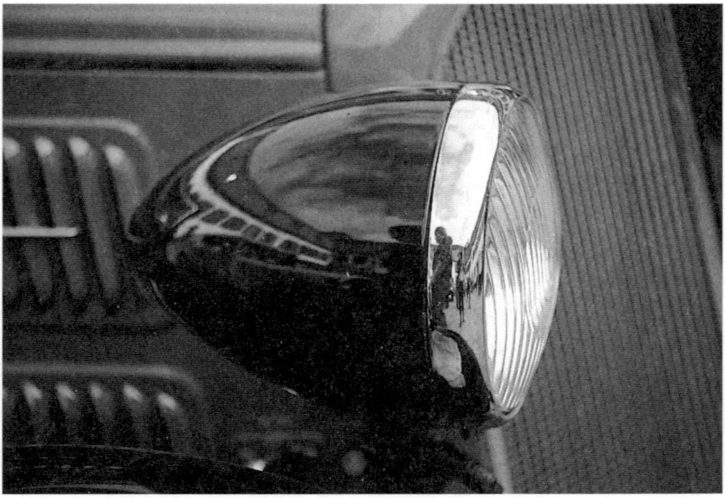

Subjects which are all black will deceive most exposure meters. If black is to appear black, a minus compensation is necessary. On manually-controlled cameras this is achieved simply by closing the aperture or increasing the shutter speed.

Calculating the correct exposure is a simple matter of aligning a pointer with a marker resulting in a suitable light value. Afterwards the required shutter speed/aperture combination can be read off a scale.

Further up the price scale is the Gossen Multisix exposure meter recommended for all those Nikon F users who occasionally need to solve more unusual metering problems and who may work in a studio with a small flash system. The metering and indicating area extends from EV -4 to EV17 and $^1/_{4000}$ sec to 8 hrs as well as f/0.7 to f/128, making the Multisix really secure for the future - and this also applies to a film speed range from ISO 0.8/0° to ISO 100000/51°. Even when trying to push high-speed black-and-white films to the impossible the Multisix can calculate the correct shutter speed/aperture combination and this can be set - as far as technically possible - on the Nikon F.

Of course, the Multisix can either meter the light reflected from the subject or the light falling on the subject. Wherever possible you should go for metering the incoming light as this is not influenced by any shiny, highly reflective or matt, low reflecting areas of the subject. The light metering therefore will give you a neutral result. Only very dark or very light subjects are excluded from this method and exposures must be corrected with a plus or minus compensation when such subjects are involved.

Flash metering is also possible with the Gossen Multisix. Although this is no real substitute for the TTL metering and control of modern SLR cameras such as the Nikon F-801 or F4, in a small home studio where the occasional macro or table top picture is taken this type of metering is a must.

The large LCD display of the Gossen Multisix certainly simplifies reading off the values.

Exposure Control - entirely manual

No matter which finder is attached to your Nikon F - standard prism, Photomic FTN, sports or waist-level - shutter speed and aperture must be set by hand.

The setting of the aperture has nothing to do with the camera itself, of course, but is dependent on the lens fitted to the Nikon F. An important point in this context is that even on this camera, lenses with automatic apertures can be used. To avoid misunderstanding this does not mean aperture control by the camera.

An automatic iris means that you can manually set an f/number on the aperture ring of the lens without the aperture closing inside the lens. When your exposure meter calculation suggests a combination, for example, of $^1/_{125}$ sec and f/8 for a particular situation you can set f/8 on the lens but still look at the subject through the bright viewfinder. Only pressing the shutter release button or the depth of field preview button closes the aperture to the selected value, which opens again after

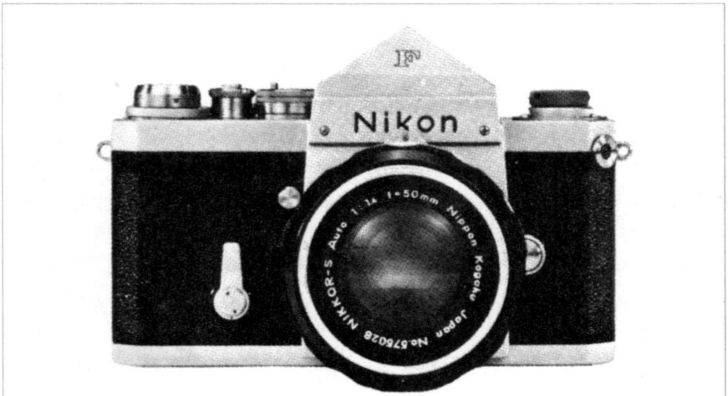

The Nikon F with the standard prism. Its few controls are arranged clearly and practically. A professional camera isn't made by a multitude of buttons and switches, but by its robustness and ability to adjust to different tasks.

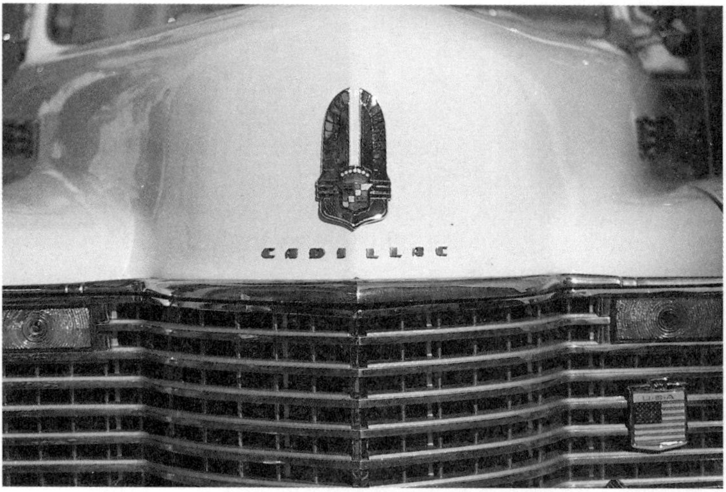

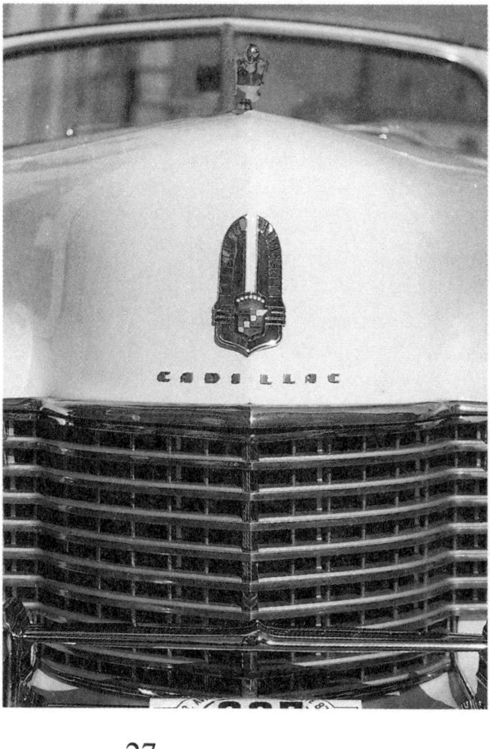

Once exposure metering has taken place, aperture and shutter speed of a manually controlled camera can be selected and used for a whole series. The change from landscape to portrait format has no effect on the exposure, even if a piece of sky suddenly appears in the shot.

exposure or when the depth of field preview button is released. Nowadays an automatic iris is not topical any more but when the Nikon F was introduced this type of aperture was new.

Preselection of the aperture not only has a bearing on the exposure it also influences the extent of the depth of field. The wider the aperture the smaller the depth of field, which increases with stopping down. A look through viewfinder and lens with full aperture therefore shows the subject always with the smallest possible depth of field. In the case of portrait photography with a wide aperture medium telephoto the viewfinder image depicts the portrait against a blurred background - while with f/5.6 or f/8 irritating background details are quite evident.

The depth of field preview button can help to avoid such unwelcome surprises. This button is located on the front of the camera on the right-hand side of thelens and can easily be operated with the index or middle finger of the right hand. When pressed, the aperture closes to the preselected value and you can assess in the darkened viewfinder how the picture is made up of focused and unfocused areas.

When using the depth of field preview button it is not advisable to release the shutter at the same time as the mirror would be blocked. Although you can release it again by operating the film rewind knob and shutter release button you will invariably lose a shot.

The optical evaluation of the depth of field in the viewfinder is theoretically possible with all apertures featured by the attached lens. In practice, however, you are likely to find that f/8, for example, is too dark for precise control of the depth of field. In this case you could still read off the extent of the depth of field from the scale on the lens.

Beside the aperture the shutter speed is the second component in exposure control. The Nikon F already features a shutter made from titanium foil, a very light

Compared to almost all other SLR cameras, the shutter release button is located surprisingly far back. The 'A' and 'R' markings refer to film transport. Apart from the 'B' setting still used nowadays, the shutter speed dial also has a 'T' setting.

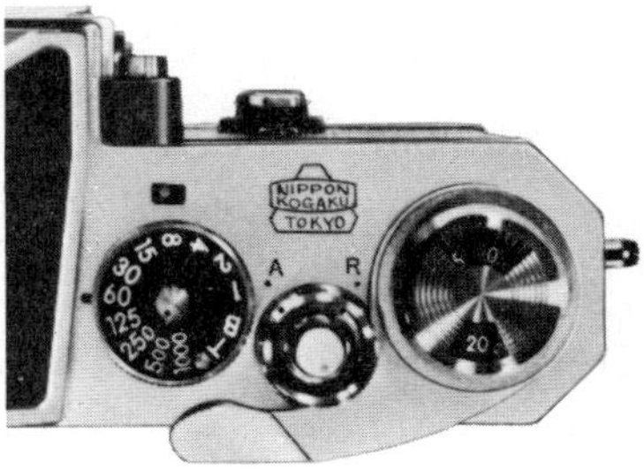

and robust material. This provides speeds from 1 to $^1/_{1000}$ sec. Taking into account the speed ranges from 30 to $^1/_{8000}$ modern cameras offer, the 11 speeds of the Nikon F seem rather modest.

But the absence of ultra-fast speeds is no reason to spurn the Nikon F. Of course, there are subjects that are best captured with $^1/_{4000}$ or $^1/_{8000}$ sec but these instancies are so rare that such fast shutters need not have been developed especially for them. The reason for the very fast shutter speeds lies rather in the efforts of the designers to produce shutters with fast sync speeds. To be able to use a flash with $^1/_{200}$ or $^1/_{250}$ sec is indeed an advantage. The sync speed of $^1/_{60}$ sec offered by the Nikon F is not that fantastic but it has been a popular shutter speed for electronic flash units for decades. As these flashes were not as widespread as they are today the Nikon F can be set to work with different flash bulbs, and with the slow burning FP bulbs you can even make flash exposures with $^1/_{1000}$ sec.

The absence of slow shutter speeds on the other end of 1 sec should not really be a disadvantage as the Nikon F offers the "B" and "T" settings to control slower shutter speeds.

When the shutter speed selector dial is turned to "B" the shutter opens when the shutter release button is pressed and it closes when the button is released. This is usually easier when a cable release is attached. The

Nikon F has no cable release connection inside the shutter release but an external thread around the shutter button. This is rather rare today but your dealer should be able to provide a suitable adaptor so that any ordinary cable release can be used with the Nikon F.

If you decide on the "T" setting the shutter is opened by pressing the shutter release and you finish the exposure by turning the shutter speed selector dial away from the "T" setting. This is quite a delicate operation as the picture could be spoiled through camera shake. When you finish a five-minute exposure of a low lit subject, however, a tiny movement of the camera lasting only a fraction of a second should have no adverse effect.

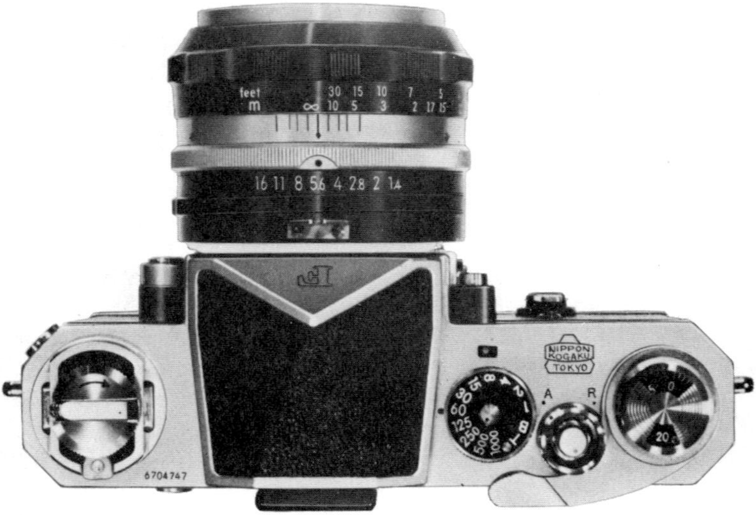

The basic version of the Nikon F is a simple camera which is easily mastered. As the viewfinder is interchangeable, the accessory shoe is located around the edge of the rewind knob - an impractical position but not changed until the Nikon F3.

Features - the bare necessities

Some of the features of the Nikon F have already been described: the interchangeable viewfinder prism with its release button, the shutter speed selector dial with "B" and "T" settings, the shutter release with external thread for a cable release, the depth of field preview button - but this, of course, is not all.

The winding lever...
...on the top right of the camera is still a very simple one. But this makes no difference to its actual function - winding on the film and cocking the shutter at the same time.

The winding lever can either be operated in one single movement or in several small movements - which could be less obvious in certain situations. After exposure the shutter remains locked until it is cocked - and as both functions are coupled in the winding lever this means in effect that inadvertent double exposure is impossible. But how can you achieve deliberate double exposure? The solution is rather complicated but still easier than with many other cameras. You only need to turn...

The A-R ring...
...from the "A" position (film advance) to the "R" position (film rewind). Then pull out and turn...

The rewind crank...
...on the top left of the camera slowly clockwise. Keep an eye on the shutter release as it is connected to the film winding spool inside the camera. When the film is being wound on the shutter release button revolves, which can be observed quite easily by watching the small dot at its edge, ensuring proper film loading from the cassette. A deliberate double exposure can be made by turning the rewind crank until the shutter release

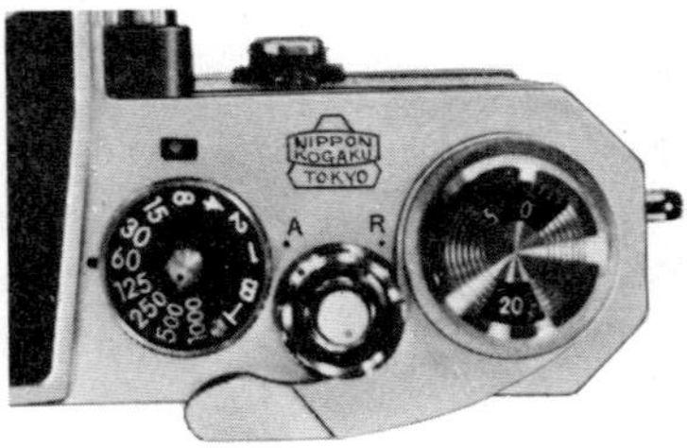

Film counter and film advance lever form one unit. There is also a small window which indicates the film length - in case you forget to set the correct number when loading the film.

has revolved by one turn. Now the film has been moved backwards by 1 frame and the last exposed frame lies to the right of the film window. When the winding lever is now operated this already exposed frame is brought into the exposure position a second time and at the same time the shutter is cocked. If you also have an interesting second subject and watch the exposure, nothing should go wrong now. It is possible, however, that the second frame does not align with the first one but is slightly offset. This is no problem for ordinary double exposures but could be annoying for *doppelganger* pictures.

The frame counter...
...on top of the winding lever is only reset to zero when the camera back is opened, otherwise it counts forwards with each winding of the film. Therefore, after a double exposure you can take an additional picture to the figure indicated by the frame counter. The counter counts forwards.

When a loaded Nikon F is not used for a while and you want to know how many frames are left or whether a black-and-white or colour film is loaded and what speed it is, there are two reminders on the Nikon F.

The film load reminder...
...like the frame counter is located in the winding lever. By moving a small pin you can see the desired frame number in a small window.

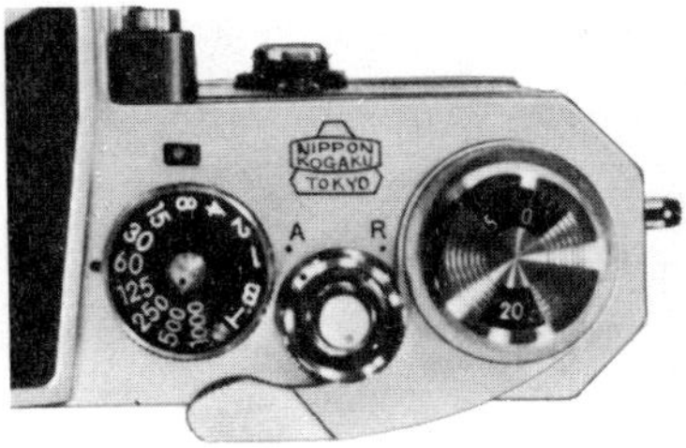

The shutter speed dial also doubles as the flash synch selector. The relevant symbol appears in the small indicator window. The frame counter and film load rewinder dial are incorporated in the winding lever.

The film speed reminder dial...
...is located at the bottom of the camera body. This dial is engraved with film speeds from ISO 25/15° to ISO 1600/33° in whole increments plus "E" for empty. The dial can be turned so that one of the numerals faces a black or red index, black for black-and-white films and red for colour. If you need more indexes you could make extra markings with indelible ink. But be careful; when an exposure meter is attached to the Nikon F the film speed setting on the reminder dial has no bearing on the operation of the meter. In this case just use it as a reminder.

The flash sync selector...
...is operated by lifting and turning the shutter speed dial. Although there is a choice of four different settings, shown in the window in front of the shutter speed dial, you are most likely to need the "FX" setting for synchronizing electronic flash units. The flash can be used for $^1/_{60}$ sec and all slower speeds. The other settings on the sync selector concern different types of flash bulbs.

The "oF" setting is for sync speeds of $^1/_{30}$ to 1 sec and "B" is for FB, M and MF class flash bulbs. The "o<dark>" setting is for $^1/_{60}$ sec for class FB and M flash bulbs and the "o<light>" setting is for a speed of $^1/_{125}$ sec for class M bulbs with bayonet (not "M" miniature bulbs) plus $^1/_{1000}$ to $^1/_{125}$ sec for class FP bulbs.

If an exposure meter is fitted to the Nikon F it must be removed when a flash is used.

The accessory shoe...
...of this camera is found on top of the rewind knob. Only special flash units can be attached and coupled with it. Flash units with a conventional camera connection must be used with an adapter.

The film rewind knob...
...is large and thus easy to operate even with gloved fingers. A small arrow points in the direction the knob has to be wound. The rewind knob also serves to verify that you have loaded the film correctly. When the winding lever is operated the rewind knob must revolve and if, despite the film reminder, you are not sure whether there is a film in the camera you only need to turn the rewind crank carefully in the direction of the arrow. If you can feel no resistance after one or two turns the camera is empty.

The mirror lock-up...
...is a button to the right of the lens mounting (as you hold the camera). When this button is turned, the mirror will swing up. What is the purpose of this? After all, the view through the lens is the great advantage of SLR cameras and this is made possible by the mirror. The mirror should be raised first when bellows or very long focus telephotos are used for large reproduction scales and the vibrations caused by the mirror movement might be detrimental to the picture. Fix the camera and bellows or super-tele to a sturdy tripod, determine the framing, set the focus, raise the mirror and release the shutter by using a cable release. This should eliminate any danger of camera shake.

The mirror also needs to be up when certain speciality lenses such as the fisheyes 6.5mm,f/5.6 or 10mm,f/5.6 are used. These lenses project back so far

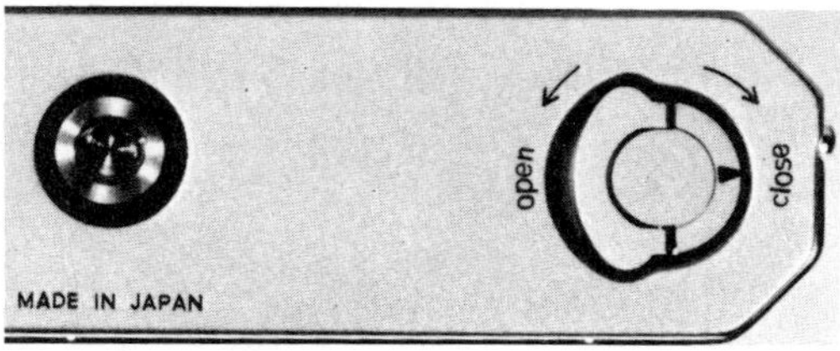

The back cover lock of the Nikon F is located on the base of the camera. The back cover is removed together with the camera base, which is why the tripod thread is fixed to the camera body and reached through a hole in the base.

into the camera body that they would obstruct the movement of the mirror and damage it.

The self-timer...
...on the right front side of the camera is used to set a timed delay before exposure. The delays possible are 3, 6 or 10 sec and can be selected by turning the lever to any of the markings on the collar of the self-timer. Any time up to a maximum of 10 sec can be used. In order to activate the delay function, however, first push the self-timer lever down and then press the small button underneath the self-timer arm. Operating the normal shutter release would expose the film without delay.

The lens lock release button...
...to the left of the lens (as you hold the camera) clicks into place when a lens is fitted to the Nikon F and turned anticlockwise. To remove the lens from the camera body, press this button and turn the lens clockwise until it can be taken out of the bayonet.

The camera back twist lock...
...is located on the bottom of the camera. Here the Nikon F demonstrates its relationship to rangefinder Nikons because unlike modern cameras, the back cover of the Nikon F does not swing open but slides off.

Thanks to the slotted take-up spool, loading the film is quite easy. The trick is to insert the film leader in one of the slots, holding it down with your thumb and then to pull the cassette to the left until it can be placed in the cassette chamber.

Accessories for the Nikon F

For the professional photographer a camera that can be adapted to different situations is of the highest importance. No wonder, then, that the three cameras that became synonyms for a professional camera - Hasselblad, Canon F-1 and the Nikon F and its successors - were built on the modular principle. Central to the modular design is the body to which viewfinders, lenses, motor drives and back covers can be attached according to requirements.

The viewfinders...

...for the Nikon F on the one hand are fixed so firmly that they can stand a few knocks from the meleé of press photographers. On the other hand they can be changed so quickly and easily that there is no need to deliberate whether the effect is worth the effort. Apart from the eye-level finder and the Photomic FTN, two other finders can be fitted to the Nikon F. The waist-level finder allows you to view the screen from above where, although the right way up, the image is reversed laterally. The reason for the correct orientation of the viewfinder image in normal SLR finders is the pentaprism which is absent from the waist-level finder. Looking into the finder from above is preferable in several situations. For instance, if you want to shoot unnoticed but not indiscriminately the camera can remain hanging from your neck and be set up without attracting attention. Close-up photography near the ground (flowers or insects) is also an area where the

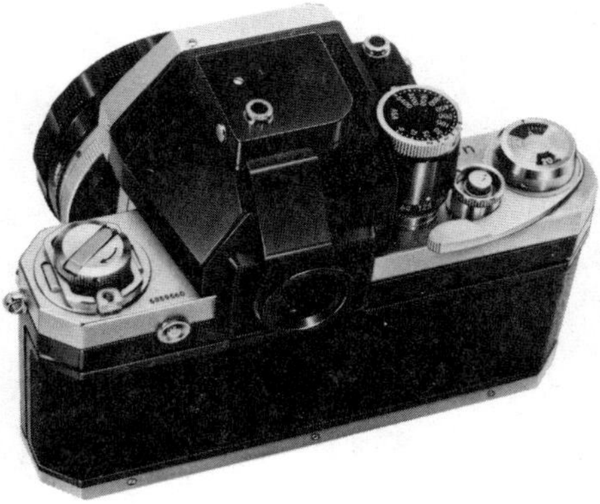

The meter needle of the Photomic head on a Nikon F can be illuminated by an clip-on illuminator to enable it to be seen better in dim lighting conditions. The release button for the viewfinder is visible to the left of the viewfinder eyepiece. The shutter speed dial of the viewfinder is mechanically coupled with that of the camera body.

need to crouch down can be very strenuous with an ordinary viewfinder - the waist-level finder makes assessing the picture and setting the lens easier. This also applies to work with a copying stand. In a crowd of people the view from above onto the screen turns into a view from below. The photographer can hold the camera above his head, is able to shoot across other photographers or spectators and still control the framing in the viewfinder. In macro photography and copying the built-in viewfinder magnifier enlarges the viewfinder image making it easier to distingguish when the image is sharp.

The action finder is a variation on the normal pentaprism finder. Viewing can either be from behind or, after angling the upper part of the finder, from above. In both cases the entire image can be seen although it appears smaller than through the ordinary prism viewfinder. On the other hand the entire image can be viewed with the eye further away, which could be of interest to the spectacle wearer - and to photographers required to wear a safety hat (cave explorers, architects and archeologists).

Focusing screens...

...that can be exchanged increase the variety of possibilities for viewing the image before exposure. There are fourteen different additional focusing screens available to the Nikon F user, plus the "A" screen fitted as standard to the camera.

The various focusing screens differ in their focusing aids designed for specific lenses or subject situations.

The A screen has a split-image rangefinder and can be used with all lenses of average focal length and for all subjects.

If you prefer microprisms to a split-image rangefinder choose the J screen which is also universally applicable - with the usual restriction for slow lenses.

If, however, you frequently use very slow lenses the G3 or G4 screens are more suitable as their large microprism area is specifically designed for such lenses. The G screen - also with central microprism - is recommended for wide-angle lenses. For architectural subjects or copying the E screen is useful as its finely-etched horizontal and vertical lines help you to align edges properly.

The M screen with a central cross was especially designed for use with bellows as the divisions along both axes enables you to calculate the reproduction scale of the exposure in the viewfinder. The four variants of the H screen are less useful as focusing performance is good but not the assessment of the subject. These screens are entirely covered with a microprism. All subject parts which are not in focus will flicker which can be quite distracting.

Motor drives...

...are accessories that make the biggest impression on many amateur photographers who see one in action. The press photographer trying to get a good shot in a milling crowd or of a moving model showing off the flow of a beautiful dress appreciates the convenience of

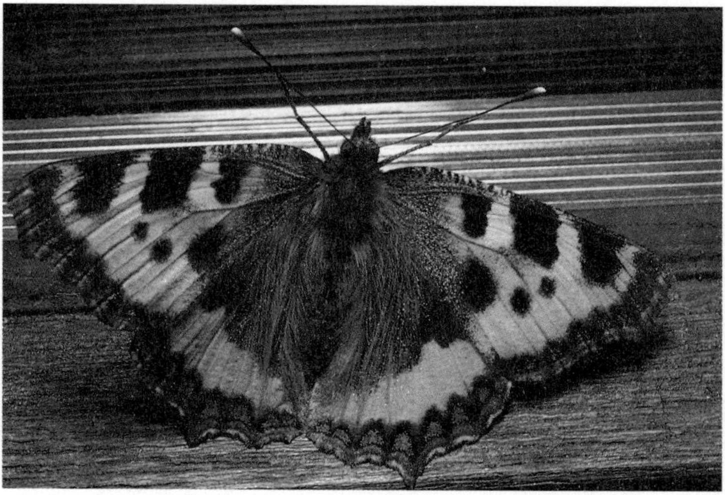

A photograph like this can be taken quickly with a zoom lens in macro setting. A winder or motor drive on the camera enables you to take a quick second and third shot without having to move and possibly chasing away the subject.

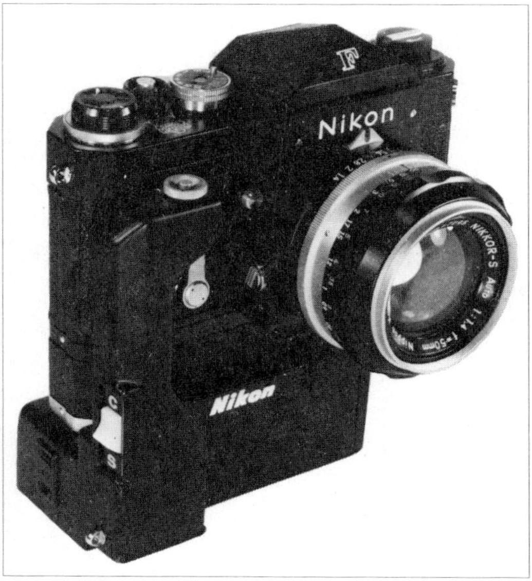

The F-36 motor drive is a relic from the old days of Nikon F cameras. With motor and exposure metering viewfinder (not shown) the camera becomes an impressive 'monster'.

being able to shoot picture after picture without the need to take the camera from the eye when the Nikon F is fitted with Motor F36. Other professionals, however, prefer to dispense with a motor drive when specialising in still subjects such as architecture or landscape.

Motor F250 is designed for use with the 250-Exposure Film Cassette and is therefore primarily suitable for scientific photography where a series of tests needs to be captured in a series of pictures.

Nikkormat EL - Beginning of Automatic Functions

The foundation laid down with the Nikon F in 1959 proved to be a solid base for a great camera system which was continually increased. Next to the professional cameras Nikon F and Nikon F2 which appeared on the market in 1971, came the Nikkormat models aimed at the dedicated amateur but which also found many friends among the professionals. In 1972 the first Nikon SLR camera featuring automatic exposure appeared. Many Nikon fans were shocked as they wanted to decide speeds and apertures for themselves. But those photographers who preferred to think before judging were very pleased with the Nikkormat EL.

Like the preceding Nikkormat cameras the Nikkormat EL differs on two major points from the professional cameras Nikon F and Nikon F2; the viewfinder is not interchangeable and it is also impossible to attach

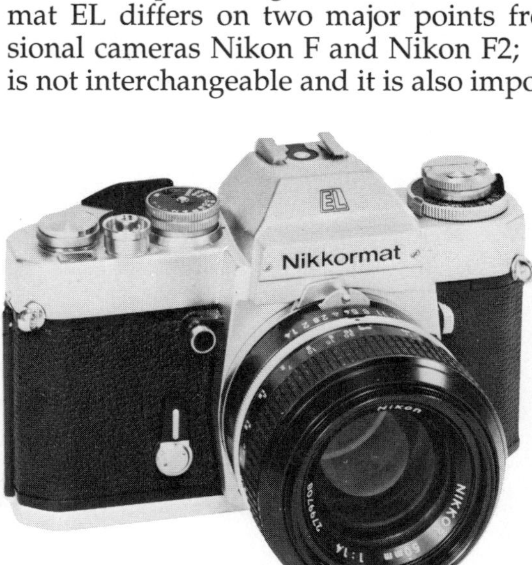

With the Nikkormat EL, Nikon enters the market of automatic exposure SLR cameras. A depth of field preview button is important in aperture priority mode - it is located to the left (seen head-on) of the slightly protruding lens mount.

a motor drive to the earlier ones. In 1976 the Nikkormat ELW was introduced which was based on the EL but featured a winder, although this wound on the film at fewer frames per second than a true motor drive.

TTL Exposure Metering - metering what you can see

The Nikkormat EL is fitted with a built-in exposure meter which meters the exposure through the lens with full aperture. The metering cell is a CdS cell which alters its electrical resistance depending on the incoming light. To evaluate this alteration it must be powered - that means the exposure meter can only function when the camera is fitted with a battery (6V silver oxide). Apart from exposure metering the battery also powers the electromagnetic shutter control.

Filters don't make good shots simply by being there, but they can be used to intensify the effect of a shot. The evening mood seen from the Ferris wheel was intensified with a warm tone filter from the Cokin range. (The filter was originally meant to improve the reproduction of skin tones in portrait shots.) A softfocus attachment was used for the shot of autumnal trees.

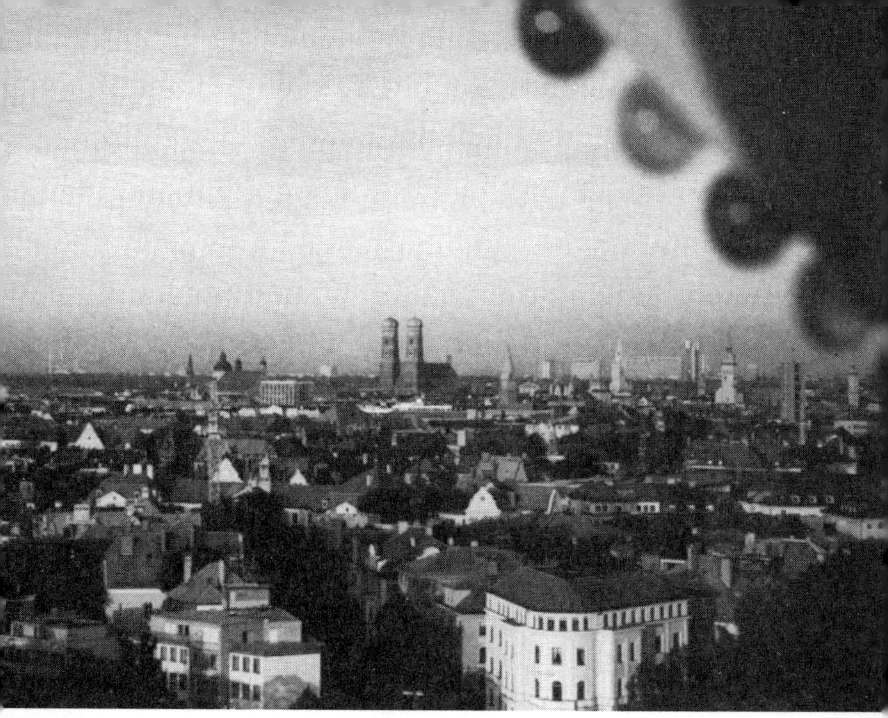

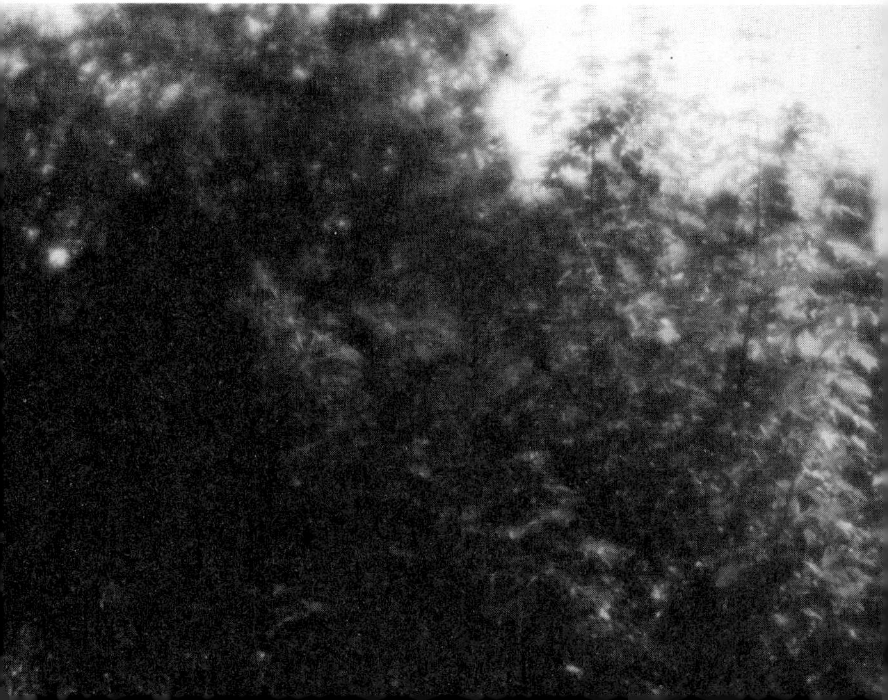

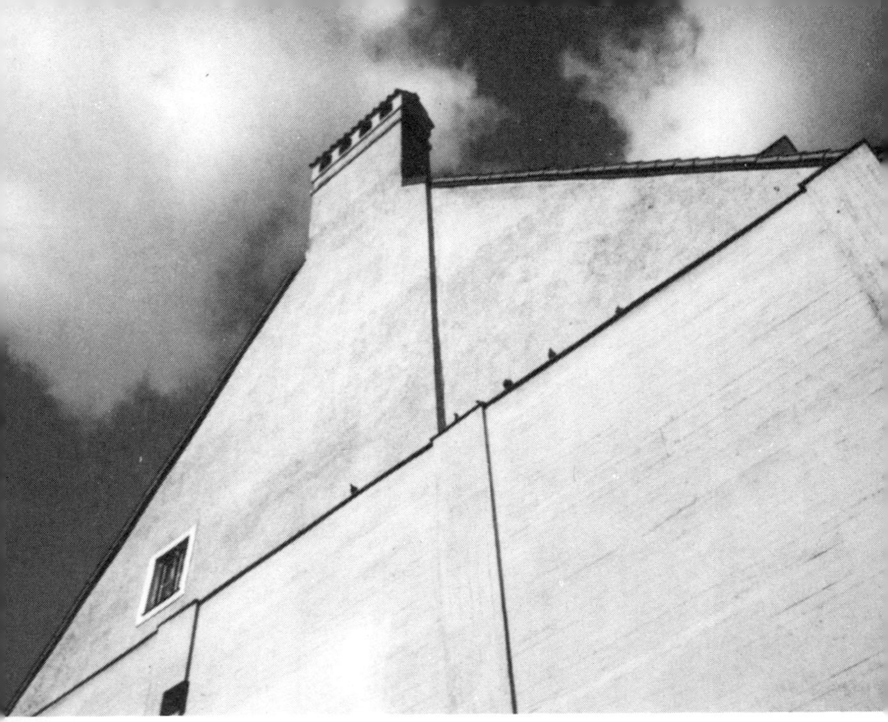

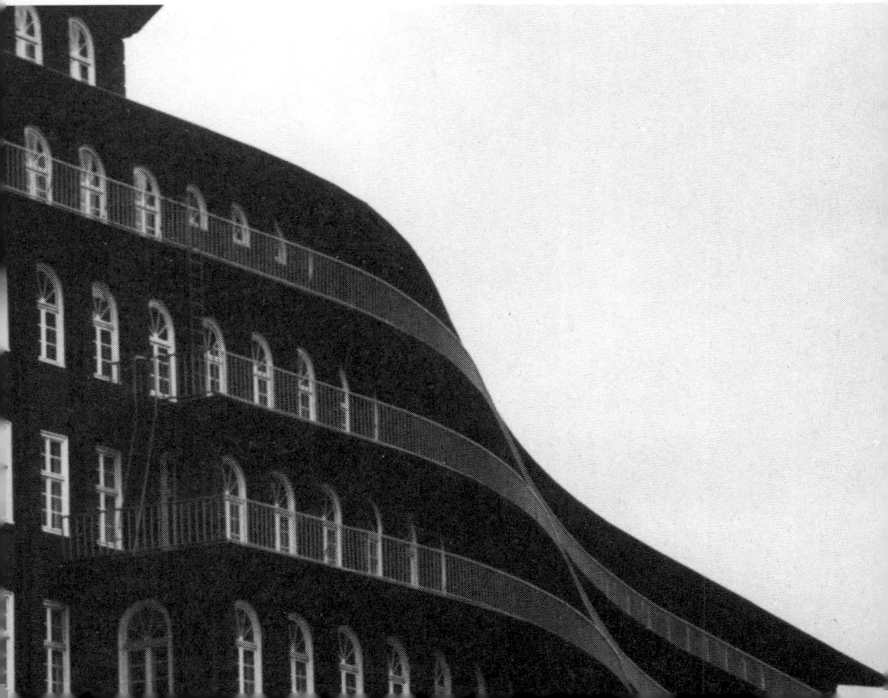

The advantages of internal metering are obvious. Metering through the lens (TTL) only includes that part of the surroundings which makes up the subject. The metering angle is therefore wider when a wide-angle lens is used, and smaller when a telephoto is used.

In only a few cases does the subject fill the entire frame. More commonly the main subject is smaller than the frame and arranged before a background which is not actually required for correct exposure. Another possibility is that although the subject fills the frame it may have too much contrast and could fool an exposure meter.

Even everyday buildings can serve as subjects if you make the most of the possibilities of wide-angle lenses and try to use the steeply converging lines they can produce as creative elements in the shot. Hamburg's Chile House is effective in itself, so it is only a matter of selecting the image section in such a way that the graphic structure is emphasised. In this case a tele zoom helps.

Centre Weighted Metering - typically Nikon

Right from the beginning Nikon designed exposure metering in such a way that the result would favour the centre of the picture more than the edge - this already applied to the Photomic metering finders for the Nikon F and F2. But this alone is nothing special as centre weighted integral metering with the emphasis on an undefined zone in the middle of the picture was also offered by other manufacturers. Nikon, however, defined exactly which area would be emphasised more for exposure metering by a fine clearly-visible circle of 12mm diameter on the focusing screen

The brightness of the subject area inside the circle influences the metering by 60% while the rest is metered at 40%. In practice this means that the exposure meter of the Nikkormat EL enables you to work quickly and precisely.

When the subject is made up in such a way that the important parts are found in the centre anyway, or when it is evenly lit and not with too much contrast,you

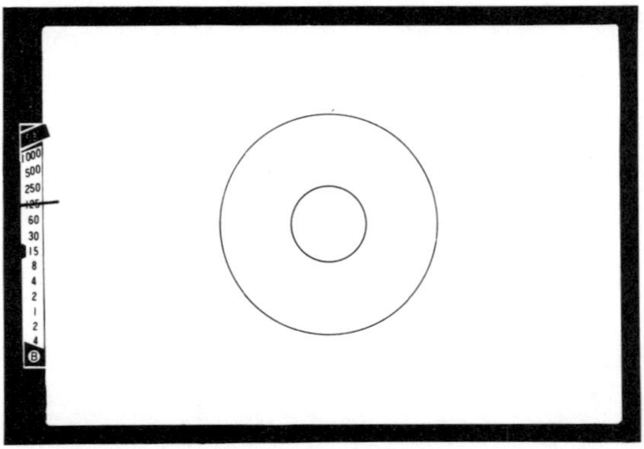

The circle in the focusing screen clearly shows which part of the shot is weighted more (at 60%) and which less (at 40%) during exposure metering.

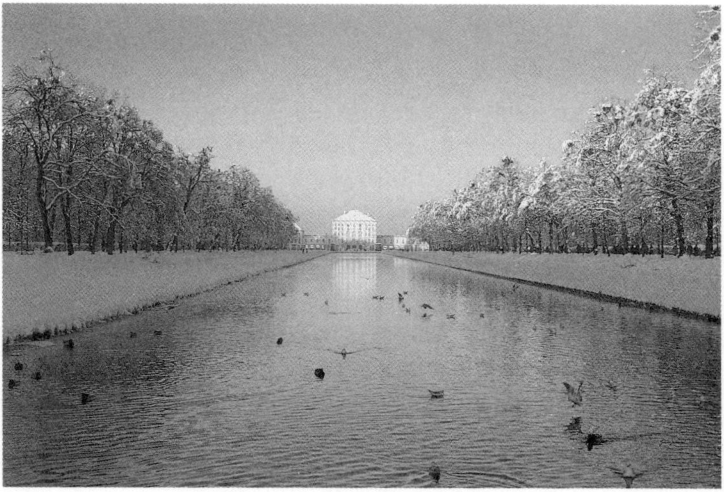

The bright sky, sunlit trees and bright building influence the exposure meter to select a brief exposure. A slight plus compensation added further detail to the shady river bank.

simply determine the framing and switch on the exposure meter by pulling out the film advance lever until a red dot is visible on the top plate. The exposure meter is now activated and you can rely on it for the ensuing exposure - whether shutter speed and aperture are set manually or automatically.

When the main subject is not in the centre of the picture or when there are strong contrasts the exposure meter of the Nikkormat EL still achieves good results. Just make sure that in the first case the main subject fills the central metering circle, adjust the exposure accordingly - manually or automatically - redetermine the framing and release the shutter.

In order to get the main subject into the central metering circle you can either go closer to the subject or you can bring it forward by using a longer focal length for metering purposes. This is easily done with a zoom lens. When there are strong contrasts - very bright patches next to very dark ones - you could try to exclude the bright and dark elements from the metering and aim the metering circle towards a subject part with average brightness.

If that is not possible either, find a substitute subject for the actual subject. The palm of the hand of an average Middle European, not too tanned, meets this requirement quite well, especially if you add half a stop as well. This would bring a better exposure than that metered from a subject rich in contrasts. A medium grey stone wall or perhaps even a grey photo bag would make good substitute subjects. Just try it and make a few corrections if necessary. Obviously it is important when using a substitute subject that the light is the same for both cases.

Open Aperture Metering - metering with full aperture

Exposure metering with full aperture has the advantage that the subject can be seen and assessed in the viewfinder right until the exposure is made.

The aperture remains open - the value set on the aperture ring is irrelevant. Only when the shutter is released or the depth of field preview button is pressed, does the aperture close to the value set. In order for full aperture metering to function the camera needs to know the size of the largest aperture.

Information about the focal length is passed to the Nikkormat EL manually - and all Nikons up to 1977 when AI lenses appeared - when the lens is attached. First set the aperture ring to f/5.6 and then fix the lens to the camera, ensuring that the meter coupling prong of the lens engages with the meter coupling pin at the top of the bayonet. Fasten the lens by turning it lightly in a clockwise direction, then first set the aperture ring to the smallest aperture and then to the largest. This action programs the camera for open aperture metering.

With some accessories such as preselection lenses, bellows or extension rings open aperture metering is not possible. In that case the iris diaphragm in the attached lens is closed to the correct value at which the exposure should take place, unless you want to utilize the small depth of field of the largest opening.

The exposure meter receives the light coming through the closed aperture into the camera and calculates the required exposure.

And there are various ways of achieving correctly exposed pictures depending on the type of lens or accessory attached.

Exposure Control - relying on automatic control is not all bad

In the 70s every camera featuring automatic exposure gave cause for lengthy discussions. Should a dedicated photographer rely on automatic exposure? If yes, on which? Shutter speed priority or aperture priority?

Looking at the matter in more detail we know that in order to have a correctly-exposed picture we need to meter the light. We already know how to meter the light with the Nikkormat EL. What happens is as follows:

The exposure meter determines the brightness of the subject and relates this to the film speed, manually set from between ISO 25/15° to ISO 1600/33°. From both data - subject brightness and film speed - we reach the value by which exposure should occur. This exposure value is made up of the shutter speed and aperture combinations which all lead to the same exposure. The exposure value 13 for ISO 100/21° looks like this, for example:

f/32 and $^1/_8$ sec
f/22 and $^1/_{15}$ sec
f/16 and $^1/_{30}$ sec
f/11 and $^1/_{60}$ sec
f/8 and $^1/_{125}$ sec
f/5.6 and $^1/_{250}$ sec
f/4 and $^1/_{500}$ sec
f/2.8 and $^1/_{1000}$ sec
f/2 and $^1/_{2000}$ sec
f/1.4 and $^1/_{4000}$ sec
f/1 and $^1/_{8000}$ sec

Which combination is used depends, of course, on the technical design of the camera. On the Nikkormat EL with a Nikkor 50mm,f/1.4 the limit is f/8 as this standard lens cannot be stopped down any further, and f/1.4 is the second limit as there is no other aperture available. Finally $^1/_{1000}$ is another limit as the Nikkormat EL has no faster shutter speed. Above these limits the exposure can only be controlled by the one factor that still offers some scope, i.e. the film speed.

Once you have achieved an exposure value you can manually set any one of the speed/aperture combinations.

You can also rely on automatic exposure. Set the shutter speed dial to the A position and preselect an aperture. The camera immediately selects the corresponding shutter speed - as long as there is one available. As soon as a new aperture is selected the camera adjusts the shutter speed to the new aperture value. If, for example, your Ektachrome 100 requires EV13 for correct exposure you preselect f/8 and the camera sets the only available suitable shutter speed - $^1/_{125}$ sec. If, however, you have selected f/2 the camera

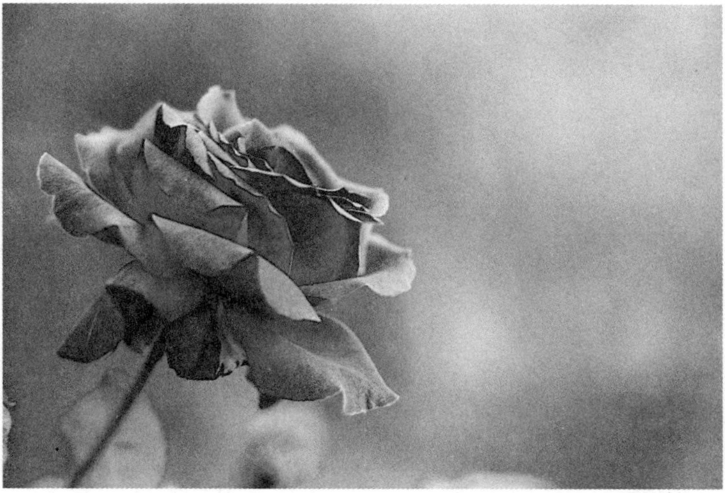

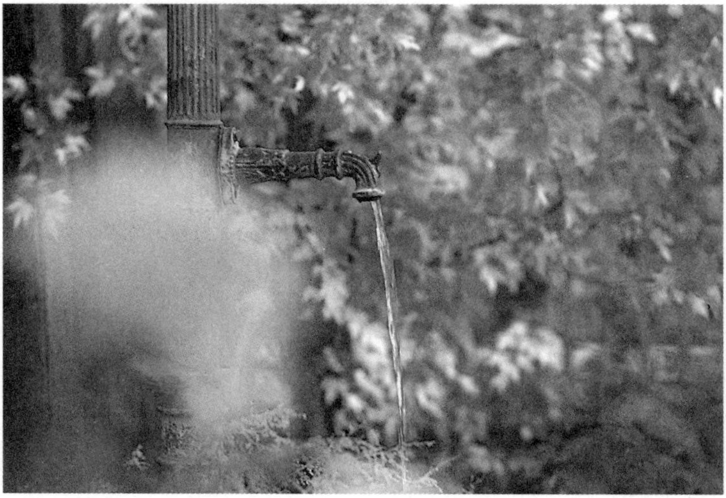

The selection of a wide aperture means a shallow depth of field which can be positioned either in the foreground or in the background. However, this has no effect on the exposure.

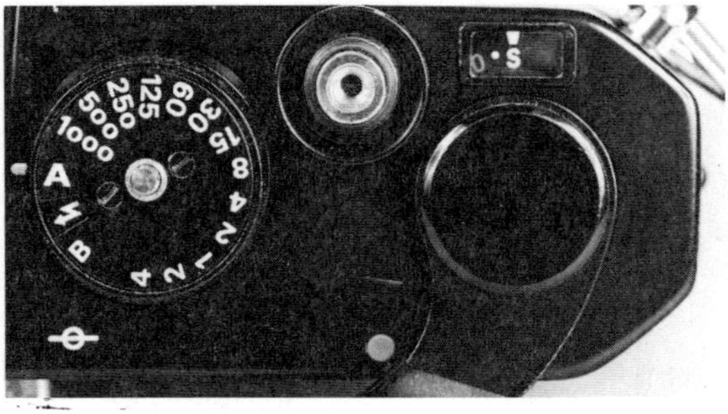

The shutter speed dial also serves as the operating mode selector. Set to 'A', the camera operates in aperture priority mode. The shutter release button can take a shutter release cable.

will warn you of impending overexposure because the Nikkormat cannot provide the required $^1/_{2000}$ sec. Its fastest shutter speed is $^1/_{1000}$ sec.

The reason for these details is to demonstrate that automatic exposure does no more than you do when you control the exposure by manually setting shutter speed and aperture. The calculations of the camera are also based on the exposure meter.

If you have metered correctly you should have a correctly-exposed picture, whether controlled manually or automatically.

Exposure Compensation - starting aid for automatic exposure

The opportunity to adjust exposure metering to a particular subject part and still utilize the advantages of automatic control is provided on the Nikkormat EL in a very simple way. The exposure meter is activated by pulling out the film advance lever. The shutter speed the camera would select according to the calculations from the exposure meter is indicated by a pointer above the shutter speed scale in the viewfinder. A wide green pointer indicates the A above the scale to the left of the viewfinder image. If the exposure needs to be corrected, aim the camera at the main subject or substitute subject. The pointer shows the new shutter

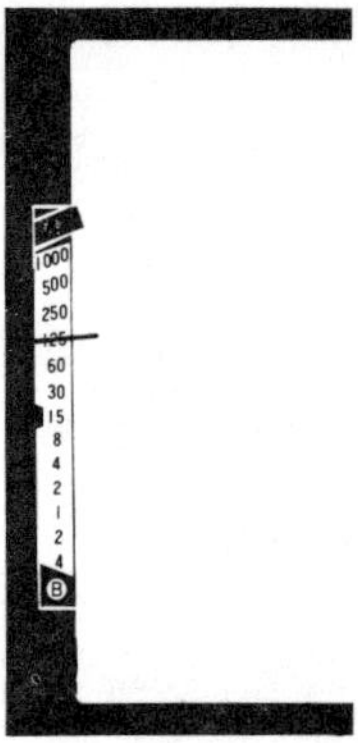

In automatic exposure, the wide pointer indicates the operating mode, the black needle the shutter speed. The two have to be brought in line for manual exposure metering.

speed which you store by pushing the self-timer/ memory lock - front right of the camera - towards the lens. When you realign the camera the pointer will again show the shutter speed the camera would select and now you can assess the degree of compensation. If you then press the shutter release the picture is exposed with the stored shutter speed and not with the one shown.

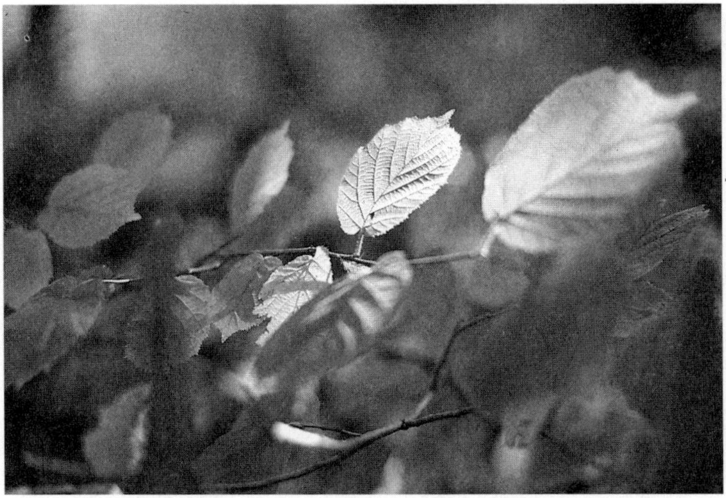

A slightly more generous exposure clearly emphasised the fresh green (this is even more obvious in the colour original).

If you are planning to make a picture series with the compensated values you should use the opportunity to set the shutter speed manually.

Manual Setting of Shutter Speed - one setting for many pictures

Press the lock in the centre of the shutter speed dial and set it to one of the engraved speeds from $^1/_{1000}$ to 4 sec. This is the same range that the camera uses automatically - except that the speeds for manual setting are available in whole stops whereas automatically they are continuously variable.

The manually-set speed is indicated in the viewfinder display by the green pointer on the speed scale while the metering index still points to the shutter speed corresponding to the ambient light, film speed and selected aperture.

The two pointers can be aligned by turning the aperture ring - the metering index changes position - by turning the shutter speed dial - the green pointer changes - or by alternating the two. Setting the correct exposure manually is rather pointless, though, as the camera can do this quicker and safer automatically.

Manual selection of shutter speed and aperture is only useful when one or two of the pictures in the series are to be intentionally exposed differently from the exposure meter calculation. If you want to make a picture series from one subject without changing the lighting and if all pictures are to be exposed slightly more generously, first set speed and aperture manually according to the exposure meter reading and then either open the aperture - whereby the depth of field decreases - or slow down the shutter speed whereby the danger of camera shake increases and the possibility arises that blurred movements appear in the picture.

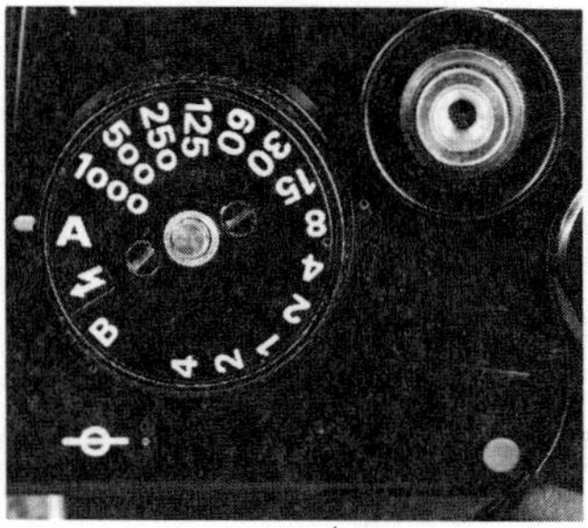

By lifting and turning the shutter speed dial at the same time, the X-synchronisation of the Nikkormat EL can be adjusted for electronic flashguns (flash symbol) and flash bulbs.

Such differing exposure can serve to avoid a false result when, for instance, a subject in the snow is to be exposed more to prevent the white of the snow showing as grey in the picture. By manually controlling the exposure it is also possible to change the effect of a picture, which although correctly exposed, would appear quite boring. A thunderstorm, for example, looks much more impressive if slightly underexposed and flower petals in the sun look more delicate when slightly overexposed.

If you are not sure by how much you want to differ from the exposure meter indication, make an exposure series. Start with the setting given by the meter and open/close the aperture or speed up/slow down the shutter speed in one, two or three increments. You must take care, however, not to fall below the hand-held limit when slowing down the shutter speed as your pictures could turn out blurred.

To vary the colour richness of a Kodachrome film, manual exposure control with full or half stops is rather too complicated. In order to adjust the film to your requirements it is better to use the film speed settings which can be varied in one-third step increments.

Manual selection of shutter speed is also necessary when the Nikkormat EL is to be used with flash. The focal plane shutter is designed in such a way that at $^{1}/_{125}$ sec or slower the second blind only starts to move when the first blind is fully open. At these speeds electronic flash can be used without the danger of the second shutter blind darkening a part of the picture. When using electronic flash, lift and turn the shutter speed dial so that a flash symbol appears in the selector window between the B and A settings, and set a shutter speed of $^{1}/_{125}$ or slower.

Flash bulbs, which are rarely used today, burn so slowly that they can also be used with faster shutter speeds than $^{1}/_{125}$ sec. If you want to use a class M, FP or MF bulb - perhaps to work in a dark room with $^{1}/_{1000}$ sec - lift the shutter speed dial and turn it until the flash bulb symbol appears between settings A and B. Afterwards any shutter speed can be selected as sync speed. The corresponding aperture is set according to the result of the guide number calculation.

Exposure Control with Working Aperture Metering - many ways to reach a result

Open aperture metering is naturally the best way to find out which shutter speed and aperture are required to expose the subject correctly because even during exposure metering the viewfinder remains bright and the subject can be seen clearly. To check the influence of the depth of field on the effect of the picture there is no need to forsake the convenience of open aperture metering. The value to which the aperture closes for the picture is, after all, the setting on the aperture ring. When you now press the depth of field preview button situated at the top right of the lens, the aperture closes to the preselected value and you can assess the depth of field down to about f/8 in the darkening viewfinder. However, with smaller apertures the viewfinder image will be too dark.

Exposure metering with open aperture is not always possible - perhaps the lens has no auto iris, or there are accessories fitted between camera and lens which are unsuitable for open aperture metering.

According to one of these reasons or whether you want to control the exposure manually or automatically there are various methods of achieving your goal through exposure metering with working aperture. If the lens has an auto iris it can be stopped down with the depth of field preview button. When the shutter speed dial is set to A the camera automatically sets the shutter speed suitable for the manually-set aperture. The speed is displayed in the viewfinder as usual.

The corresponding shutter speed/aperture combination can also be set manually by turning the aperture ring and/or shutter speed dial until the wide green pointer and the metering index are aligned. In this case pressing the depth of field preview button is not necessary.

In the case of a lens with preselected aperture, a combination of lens and bellows, or extension rings, set the shutter speed dial to A and select the aperture on the aperture ring of the lens. The shutter speed is controlled and displayed automatically. If the fastest or slowest speed is not enough the camera warns of over or underexposure. In this case select a different aperture or use a neutral density filter when the subject is too light, or a flash when it is too dark.

To avoid exposure errors it is necessary to push the coupling pin of the camera to the right before attaching a lens or accessory.

Features - almost everything catered for

The Nikkormat EL was an average camera for its time, but by today's standards rather large and heavy. Modern cameras are not necessarily smaller but they are usually fitted with a built-in motor drive.

At the top of the camera on the right, in front of the

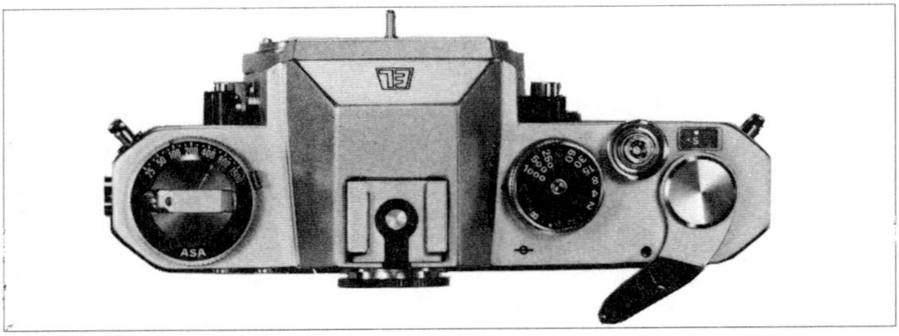

The Nikkormat EL's robust, angular body is clearly laid out. Unlike that of the Nikon F, the non-interchangeable viewfinder is fitted with an accessory shoe. The meter coupling pin is clearly visible. This engages the meter coupling prong of the attached lens.

film advance lever which also serves as the main switch and therefore should be folded to the body when not in use, is...

The frame counter...
...which counts forwards and automatically returns to 0 when the camera is opened. If you want to know, however, how many shots are still left on your film a little mental arithmetic is necessary.

The shutter release...
...is equipped with a connection for a cable release. Use a locking cable if possible, which can be operated for long exposures - a firework display or a night scene - without getting cramp in your fingers. And always use a cable release when working with a tripod.

The shutter speed dial...
...is located to the right of the view finder prism. It is used for setting the camera to automatic mode or selecting the right type of flash sync.

The accessory shoe...
...is on top of the viewfinder prism. There were no automatic features in connection with the use of flash

on the Nikkormat. To connect a hammerhead flash or other electronic flash unit the Nikkormat EL has a...

Flash sync terminal...
...on the left side of the body. Here Nikon flash cables are screwed in, other flash cables are simply pushed in.

The film speed selector dial...
...on the left of the viewfinder prism can be set from ISO 25/15° to ISO 1600/33° in one-third step increments. Low speed films with a high resolution, such as the slide film Kodachome 25 or colour negative film Ektar 25, can also be used with the Nikkormat EL. The upper limit is not quite up-to-date any more but as even the 1000 series films are rarely used in everyday photography the film speed range of the Nikkormat EL is quite adequate. By manually setting the film speed it is easily possible to adjust slide films to your own colour preferences. In order to set the film speed press the film-speed dial lock and turn the film speed dial. If you use the Nikkormat EL as well as other cameras it might be a good idea to attach a film reminder clip (by Hama) to the back of the camera containing the top of the film carton to inform you of the film loaded.

The rewind crank...
...is located on the same axis as the film speed dial. It

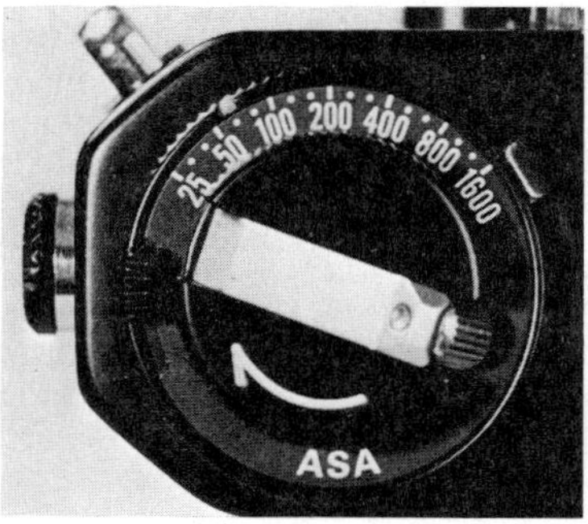

The integral exposure meter necessitates film speed input. The film speed dial is found on the left of the top plate; the rewind crank is in the centre of the rewind knob.

rewinds the film back into its cassette which need not always be at the end of its run. If you are not sure whether there is a film in the camera, carefully turn the crank in the direction of the arrow. If you cannot feel any resistance after one or two turns the camera is empty. By pulling up the film rewind knob the back cover opens. This should only be done when the film has been fully rewound into the cassette. As a safety feature the Nikkormat EL is equipped with a lock which must be pressed before the knob can be pulled up.

The battery checker...

...is located on the camera back. Pressing this button activates a light next to it, if a battery is fitted and still has power. It is important to check the battery after inserting it in the compartment underneath the mirror. Later the battery check is rather misleading. It could happen that the light indicates "OK" one moment but the next moment, after one or two shots, nothing happens and the battery has died in that short interval. After all, batteries are designed to provide nominal current for as long as possible but this goes down very rapidly towards the end of their life.

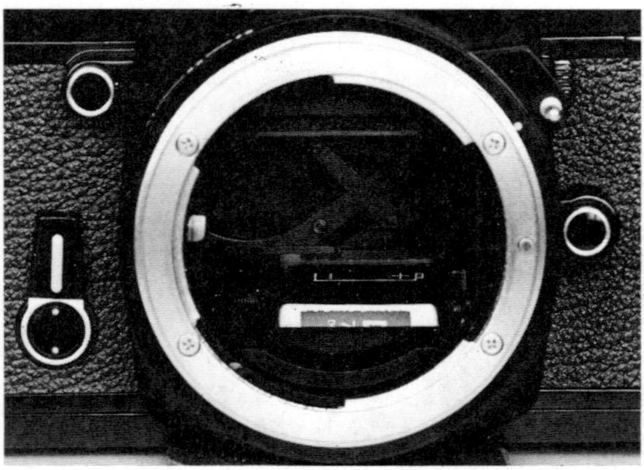

The battery of the Nikkormat EL is located in the base of the mirror housing and has to be changed through the front of the bayonet. The lens release button is located to the right of the lens mount.

The mirror lock-up lever...
...must be used whenever the 6V battery needs to be changed. This milled lever is located to the left of the bayonet and when turned upward locks the mirror in the up position. Now the battery compartment in the bottom of the mirror housing is accessible but so is the shutter. Take great care not to touch it. Apart from the battery change the mirror locking function is important when any vibration which could blur the picture needs to be eliminated. This is normally the case when working with very long telephotos and in macro photography. There are also two lenses which reach so far into the camera that they inhibit the operation of the mirror (fisheyes 6mm,f/5.6 and 10mm,f/5.6 OP). If the mirror is locked before the shot it is advisable to use the self-timer instead of the shutter release button to start exposure in order to avoid exposure errors.

The self-timer/memory lock...
...is located at the right front of the camera. Pressing the lever down activates the self-timer sequence. When pressed towards the lens the exposure metering value is stored in the camera. Above this lever is...

The depth of field preview button...
...we already know about in connection with working aperture metering and checking the depth of field.

The maximum aperture scale...
...lies to the left of the self-timer on the lens mounting and ranges from f/1.2 to f/5.6.

The rewind button...
...on the camera base is pressed before the film can be rewound into its cassette. It can also be used for double exposures although you might have a lot of waste with this technique.

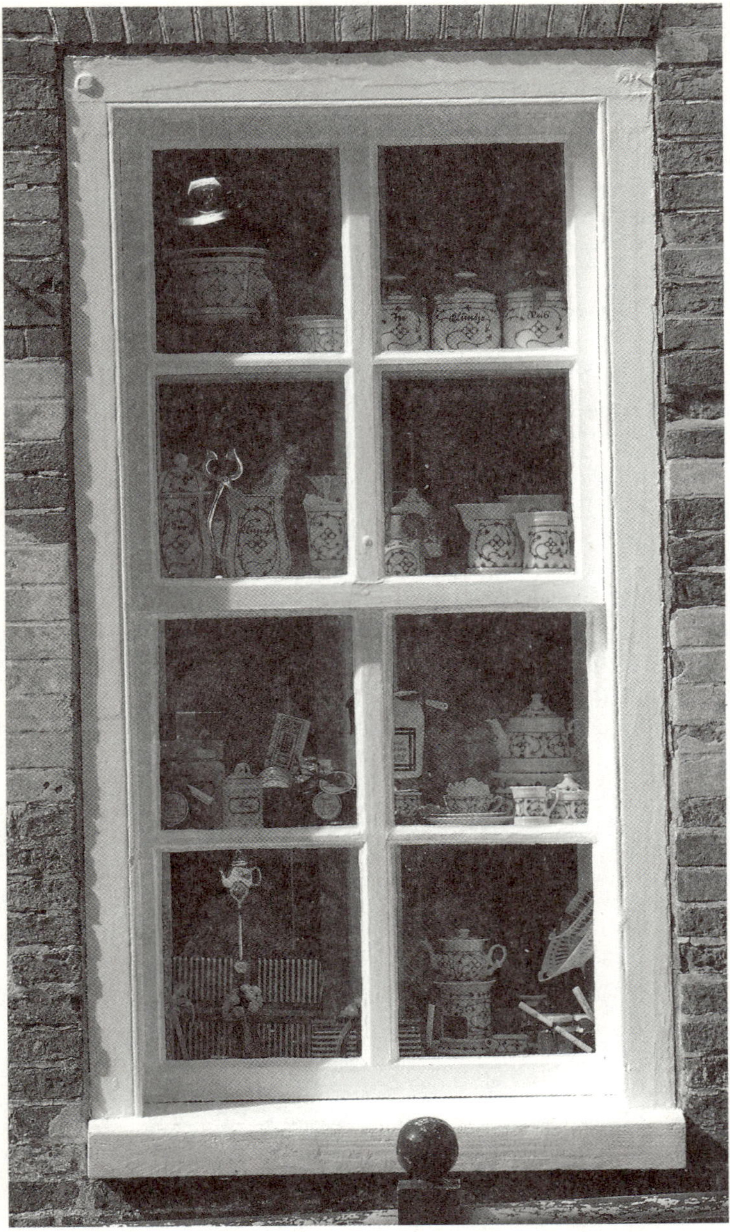

The tripod socket...

...for $^1/_4$" thread is positioned at the point of balance of the camera which obviously also depends on the type of lens attached. If a long lens features its own tripod socket this ought to be used as well.

The viewfinder...

...of the Nikkormat EL shows about 92% of the actual image. Although a 100% viewfinder is preferable as you want to see everything that will appear on the slide, say, most of the 8% missing in the viewfinder image would also disappear when the slide is framed. When a film is printed some degree of cut-off is to be expected, too.

There are also eyesight correction lenses available for fitting to the viewfinder eyepiece.

An accurate viewfinder is required to put a subject in the frame precisely where you want it. You should remember, however, that a slide frame always covers a small proportion of the image area.

Nikkormat FT2 - Solid, Simple, Clear

While the F series cameras - from the Nikon F to the F4 of today - were primarily aimed at professional photographers the Nikkormat cameras until 1977 were designed for the dedicated amateur photographer but were also used by professionals. The Nikkormat FT2 appeared in 1975 replacing the Nikkormat FTN of 1967 with a few improvements.

The body of the Nikkormat FT2 is, as was usual at the time, rather square and large. Compared to its predecessor, the FTN, its accessory shoe on top of the viewfinder was a novelty and this was the first Nikkormat camera to feature it. Another noticeable point is that the camera - like the FT and FTN - has no shutter speed dial but a shutter speed ring surrounding the bayonet, complete with shutter speed lever for ease of use.

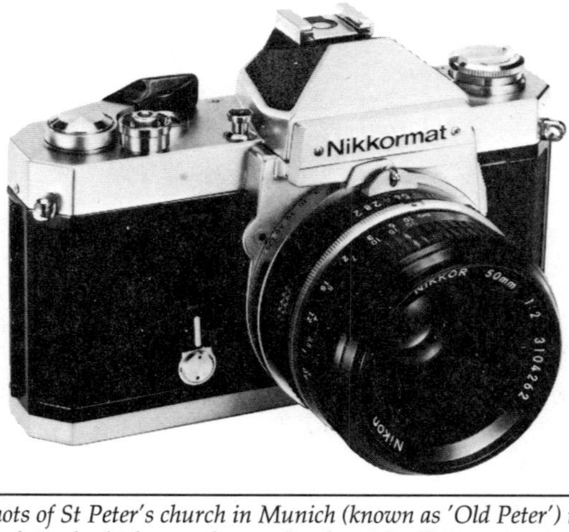

These two shots of St Peter's church in Munich (known as 'Old Peter') illustrate the performance of standard tele zoom lenses. One lens is sufficient to capture everything from an overview to a detail.

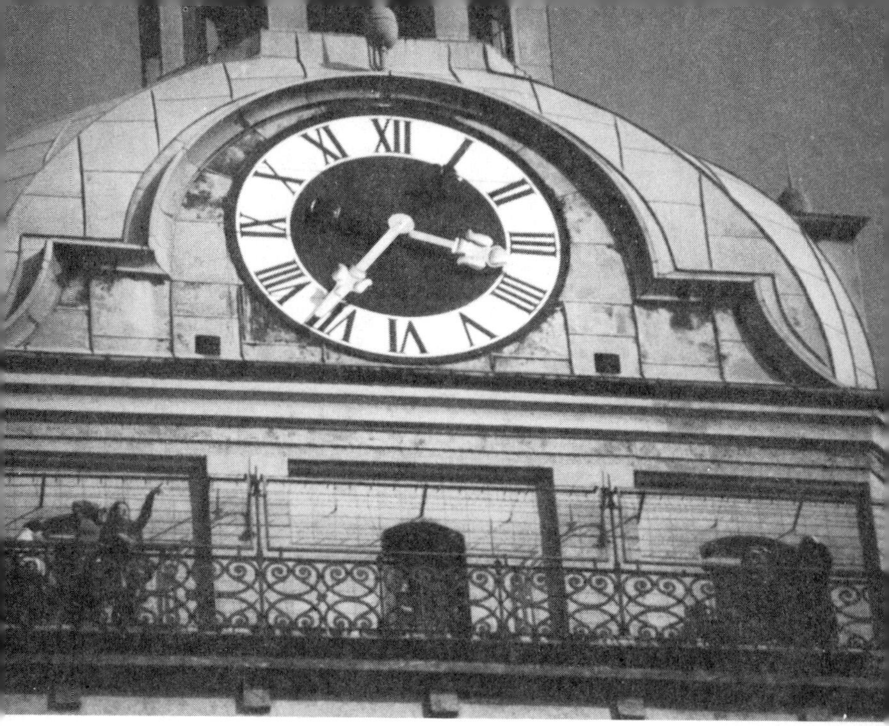

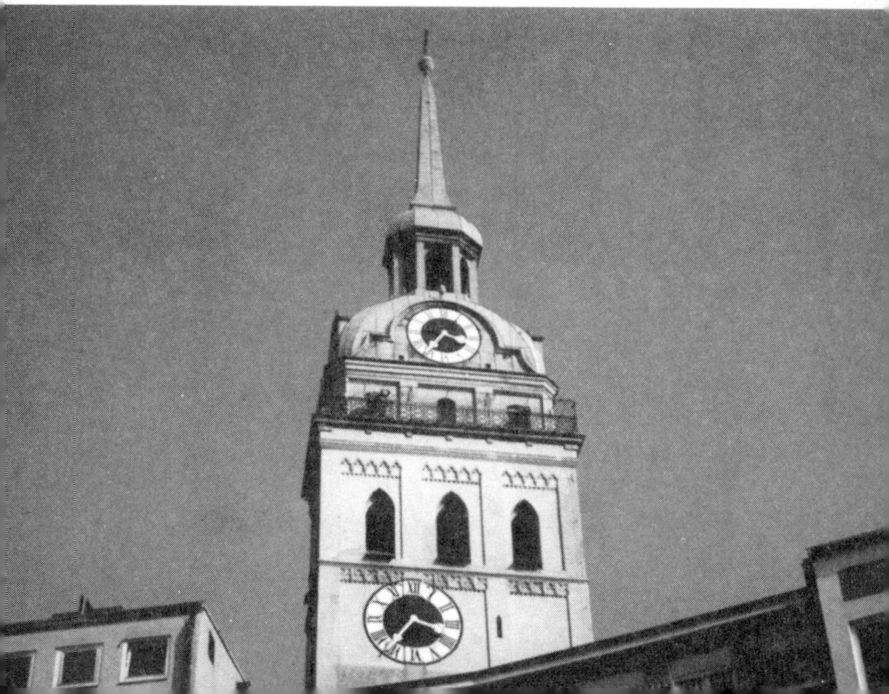

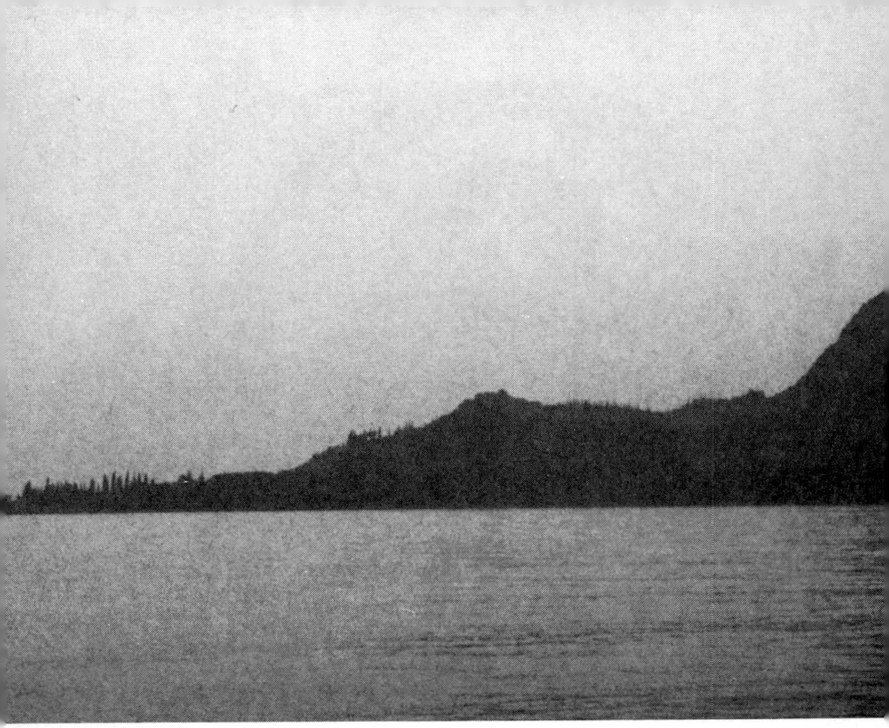

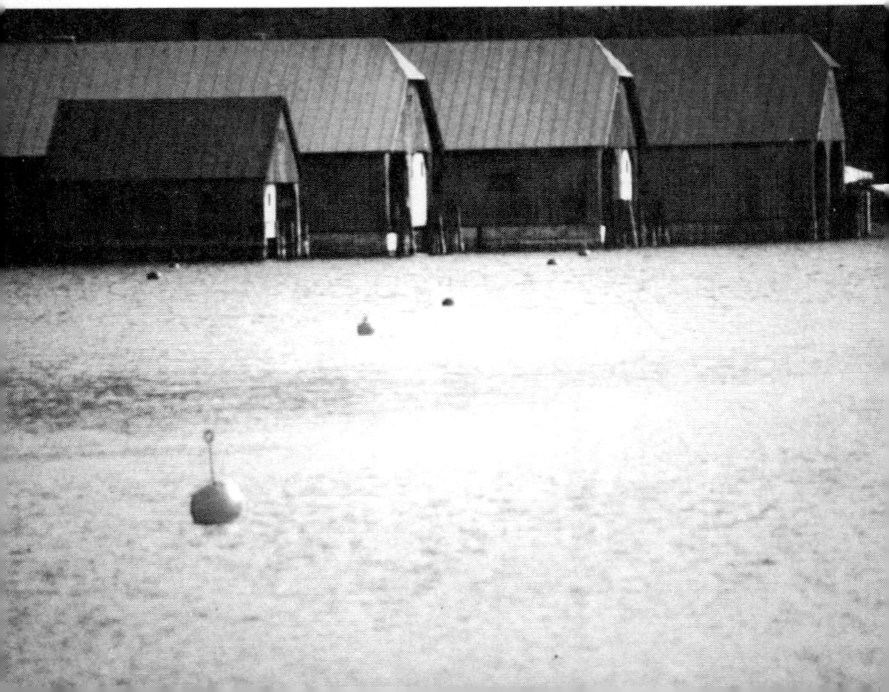

Exposure Metering - naturally with open aperture

With suitably-equipped lenses the Nikkormat FT2 offers open aperture metering. That means that the view through viewfinder and lens is normally not obscured by a closed aperture. The advantage is that the subject can be assessed accurately. The disadvantage is that when fast lenses are used the depth of field as seen through the viewfinder is very shallow. The exposure resulting from a smaller aperture could alter the appearance of the subject as foreground and background are suddenly clearly visible.

The Nikkormat FT2 also features the typical Nikon weighting for evaluation of the exposure meter result - a 12mmdiameter circle in the centre of the focusing screen accounts for 60% and the surrounding area for 40% of the metered value. The FT2 enable you to adjust the exposure very accurately for a particular subject part, especially when you use a zoom lens and decrease the angle of the TTL metering by setting a long focal length.

With the Nikkormat FT2 it is necessary to set the aperture of the lens to f/5.6, attach the lens to the camera, ensuring that the meter coupling prong engages with the meter coupling pin on the camera's bayonet. Then turn the aperture ring first to the smallest and then to the largest aperture in order to set the exposure meter to the light value of the lens. A correct setting can be checked on the focal length scale to the right (seen from the front) of the lens mounting.

Colour photographs are possible even with very little colour. This shot of a peninsula was taken on an overcast day with a telephoto lens which intensified the mist filtering the colours from the subject. The shot of boat houses is livened up and given depth by red buoys.

Exposure Control - fully manual with all its advantages and disadvantages

The correct exposure of a picture depends on the proper use of the exposure meter - not on how its metering results are converted. The exposure meter of the Nikkormat FT2 is set to an average grey value with a reflectivity of 18%. Only subjects with a lot of contrast, very light or very dark subjects, vary from this standard value and as such must be metered differently.

The exposure meter only gives the appropriate exposure value for the subject and film speed. This exposure value consists of a number of shutter speed/ aperture combinations which all result in the same exposure. Supposing you have loaded an Ektachrome 100HC or T-Max 100 and the picture is going to be taken on a bright summer afternoon, EV13 could be the right one.

EV13 consists of the following shutter speed/aperture combinations:

f/1 and 1/8000 sec
f/1.4 and 1/4000 sec
f/2 and 1/2000 sec
f/2.8 and 1/1000 sec
f/4 and 1/500 sec
f/5.6 and 1/250 sec
f/8 and 1/125 sec
f/11and 1/60 sec
f/16 and 1/30 sec
f/2 and 1/15 sec
f/3 and 1/8 sec
f/6 and 1/4 sec

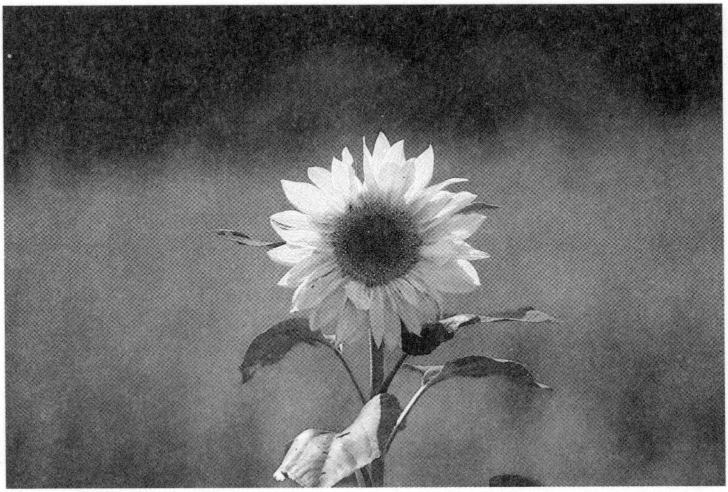

Open aperture metering shows the subject in the viewfinder with the shallowest depth of field available on the lens. If the shot is then taken with a smaller aperture, the background can suddenly appear intrusive.

Each of these combinations would in the given situation expose the film correctly - but according to the combination used it could also vary.

The fastest available shutter speed, however, is $^1/_{1000}$ sec and the smallest aperture of most Nikkor lenses is f/22 or f/32. Some can only be closed to f/16, which means that from this point of view the use of the different shutter speed/aperture combinations of EV13 is limited, too. But all the combinations between f/2.8 and $^1/_{1000}$ sec remain and - when a Nikkor 35mm f/2.8 lens is attached to the FT2 - f/22 and $^1/_{15}$ sec. The $^1/_{15}$ sec is, of course, not the slowest shutter speed as the range extends to 1 sec.

If you have set your camera to f/2.8 and $^1/_{30}$ sec and operate the shutter release, the picture will be overexposed by 5 stops. To prevent this, a metering index in the viewfinder of the FT2 warns of impending overexposure - or it indicates that the shutter speed/ aperture combination set does not correspond to the exposure value suitable for correct exposure. The meter indicator at the top left of the camera body also indicates under or overexposure.

You can now either achieve correct exposure via the aperture or the shutter speed. In the former the aperture closes to the value of f/16, in the latter the shutter speed increases to $^1/_{1000}$ sec. The unusual arrangement of the shutter speed ring and lever around the bayonet also enables you easily to adjust the shutter speed to a preselected aperture. The shutter speed can be read off the index at the top left in a hollow on the lens mounting. The aperture ring can be reached easily and changing it quickly presents no problems.

Shutter Priority? Aperture Priority? - each for its own purpose

The pointer in the viewfinder and the meter indicator on top of the camera react to a change in shutter speed and aperture. When the pointer is between the "-" and "+" and the meter indicator shows "o" the exposure is correct.

The meter indicator seems unneccessary at first as the information in the viewfinder is more important for the picture - but when shooting from ground level or with a copying stand you will appreciate it.

The cross-coupled display reacting to both aperture and shutter speed alterations allows either the aperture or the shutter speed to be preselected and the exposure adjustments to be carried out with the other factor.

When deciding on aperture priority you will have no choice but to keep checking the aperture ring of the lens as the aperture is not displayed in the viewfinder. The shutter speed selected appears underneath the viewfinder image, flanked by the next faster or slower speed.

Obviously it does not matter for correct exposure whether shutter speed and aperture correspond or whether the aperture is selected to suit a preselected shutter speed. But it does matter for the effect of the picture. The aperture together with focal length and shooting distance, i.e. the reproduction scale, determines the depth of field. The wider open the aperture the smaller the depth of field. When the aperture is closed the depth of field extends until in extreme cases it reaches from just in front of the lens to infinity.

Not only is the depth of field important to represent the subject part in front and behind the focused plane as acceptably sharp but it also greatly influences the effect of the picture.

A small depth of field enables you clearly to define the main subject and set it off against a blurred background. Portraits or pictures of flowers or leaves are particularly successful, as the unrequired surroundings have disappeared.

A large depth of field on the other hand is important for landscape or interior photography as the expanse of the landscape comes out much clearer and the room is closer to reality when some areas are not blurred.

The shutter speed determines the reproduction of movement. Fast shutter speeds freeze movement; they depict a moving subject as static. This can be useful when every detail of the subject is important. Special

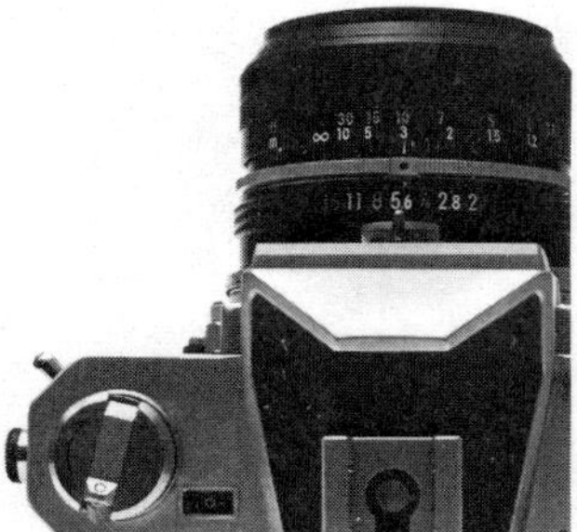

The small window of the exposure meter indicator is located between the viewfinder prism and the film advance lever. This device (a small mechanical predecessor of the LCD panels found on the top of modern AF cameras) comes into its own when taking photographs from near the ground or with the copy stand.

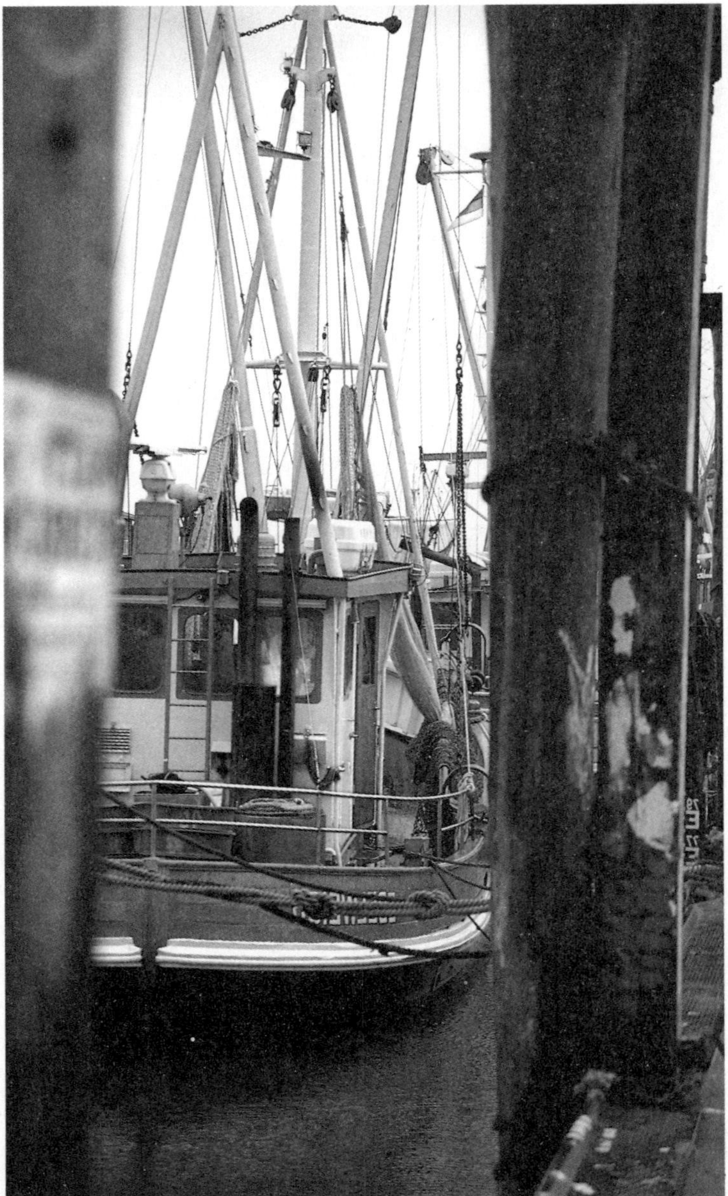

effects, too, can be achieved in this way. For example, $^{1}/_{500}$ or $^{1}/_{1000}$ sec represents the water droplets of a fountain as sparkling gems against the light, or the water of a mountain stream running over a rock appears clear and cold.

Not only is subject movement banished from the picture through fast shutter speeds - your own movements, too, can be eliminated from the picture by choosing a suitable shutter speed. Fast speeds save you from camera shake blur - the rule of thumb is "shutter speed not slower than 1 divided by the focal length in mm", if anything it should be faster. A 50mm lens with $^{1}/_{60}$ sec will not show shake nor will a 200mm lens with $^{1}/_{250}$ sec and the fastest speed for a 500mm lens should be $^{1}/_{500}$ sec if not $^{1}/_{1000}$ sec. Obviously this only applies to hand-held exposures and not when a tripod stabilizes the unit or when an electronic flash eliminates camera shake by its short length of illumination. The latter case, however, requires caution as a slow sync speed could lead to a sharp main subject but a blurred background.

A camera which can be controlled manually always gives the photographer the option of selecting either a suitable aperture, or a suitable shutter speed. In this case the aperture was selected to show the pole in the foreground out of focus, and the shutter speed was coordinated with the aperture.

In order to show movement as such in the picture you need to apply slow shutter speeds where "slow" depends on the type of movement. A racing car passing the camera in a line parallel to the film plane at 200km per hour will become blurred when exposed for $^1/_{125}$ sec. If it approaches the camera at an oblique angle, however, the unsharpness of the movement will not be evident. For a mountain stream the speed of $^1/_{125}$ sec is still fast as the water "flows" in the picture from about $^1/_{15}$ sec but at a slower speed (with tripod) the water will appear as a dense mist giving the picture a mysterious atmosphere.

Medium and slow shutter speeds can also show movement in another way - by the so-called panning method. The principle is to follow the subject - the racing car, for example - with the camera during exposure. This is a little tricky as the mirror will be up and you cannot see anything any more, but a little practice and a pan tripod should achieve good results. The slow shutter speed will become more or less ineffective through panning and the main subject appears sharp in the picture, but the background will be blurred and the illusion of movement is nearly perfect.

Features - clear yet comprehensive

The operating elements of the streamlined, rather square body of the Nikkormat FT2 are clearly arranged.

The film advance lever...

...also serves as the main switch for the exposure meter and is located on the far right of the top plate. Swing the lever outwards to wind on the film and cock the shutter. This means in effect that unintended double exposures are quite impossible. To the left, in front of this is...

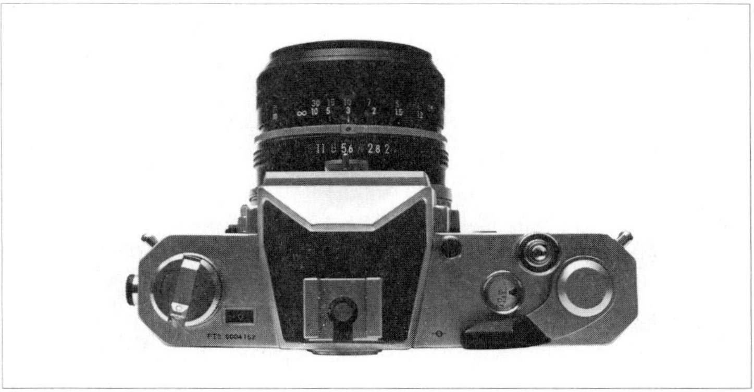

The Nikkormat FT2 makes do with few operating controls. The film plane symbol to the left of the film advance lever is clearly visible. This is of interest for macro shots - but the distance scale of the lens has to be marked very precisely and finely if the distance measured from the film plane is to be selected.

The shutter release button...

...equipped with a cable release socket for use with a tripod or copying stand. To ensure that no vibrations affect the picture the mirror can be locked up manually before exposure. Simply use the...

Mirror lock-up lever...

...to the right (seen from the front) above the lens mounting. The mirror rises by sliding this milled lever. There is only one problem with this function; should you wish to use slow speeds of $^{1}/_{2}$ sec, 1 sec or

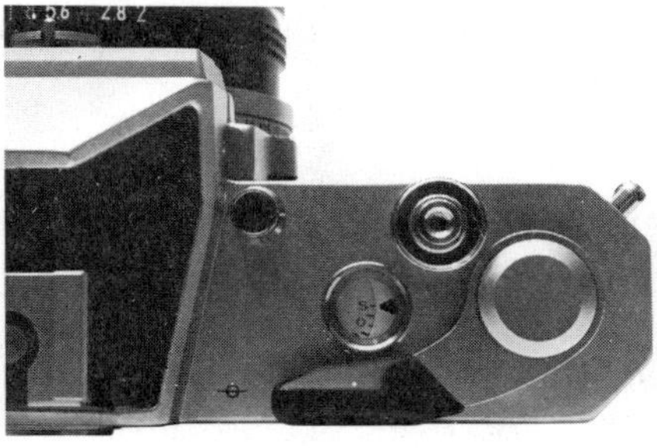

The film advance lever is at the same time the main switch for the camera. The exposure meter is activated if it is swung away from the camera body.

slower (B setting) with locked mirror the lever of the shutter speed ring and the mirror lock-up lever will be in the way.

The frame counter...
...to the left of the film advance lever, can be read very easily as the important film lengths are coloured to avoid running out of film at a critical moment.

The depth of field preview button...
...right next to the viewfinder prism is easily reached with the index finger of the right hand. Pressing this is important for checking the distribution of sharpness and blur in the picture. This can be done quite easily down to about f/8, but smaller apertures cause a darkened viewfinder image making it more difficult to distinguish between sharp and blurred areas. The depth of field preview button is also used in connection with working aperture exposure metering for lenses equipped with an auto iris. The aperture of such a lens is closed with the depth of field preview button and the light reaching the exposure meter through this opening is metered. Now you can select a suitable shutter speed. The depth of field preview button is not required for working aperture metering with bellows, extension rings, focusing aids and lenses without an auto iris as the aperture opens and closes by turning the aperture ring. Important: the coupling pin of the exposure meter must be fully pushed to the right before attaching the lenses mentioned in order to avoid incorrect exposures.

The accessory shoe...
...of the Nikkormat FT2 forms part of the camera body and is found on top of the viewfinder prism. The hot shoe does not require sync cables which is not always an advantage, however. The light from flash units sitting on top of the camera and beaming straight at the

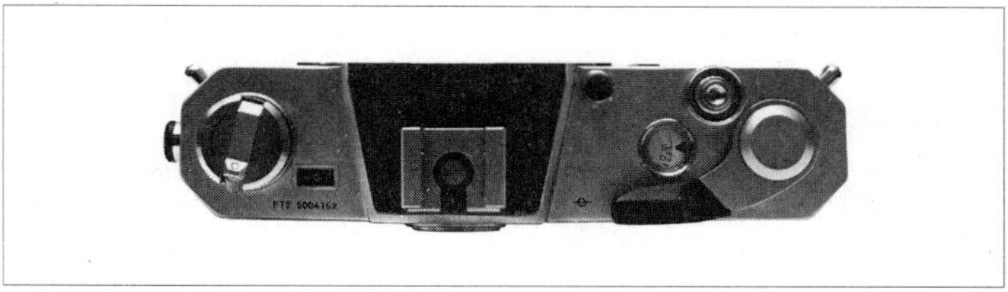

The accessory shoe of the Nikkormat FT2 has a single flash contact. At the time automatic flash modes had not yet become general. However, a computer flashgun with four computer apertures and detachable sensor, such as the Vivitar 283, facilitates convenient and reliable flashing even with this camera.

subject is flat with hard shadows. Flash units used with the Nikkormat FT2 should be equipped with a adjustable reflector so that the flash can be used indirectly. Or the light should be softened by using suitable accessories. The sync speed for electronic flash units on the Nikkormat FT2 is $^1/_{125}$ sec. In addition, all slower speeds for flash exposures can be chosen - even the B setting. Another possibility to fire a flash from the camera is...

The PC terminal...

...found on the left side of the camera body. This terminal accepts sync cables which activate flash units with cable sockets, hammerhead flash units or small flash systems. And you can still use flash bulbs with the Nikkormat FT2. Class M, FP and MF bulbs can be used with all speeds from $^1/_{30}$ to 1 sec and the B setting. Class M and FP bulbs also with $^1/_{250}$, $^1/_{500}$ and $^1/_{1000}$ sec.

The display window for exposure control...

...has already been mentioned. One more important point is that the window can be illuminated with a torch or the flame of a lighter in very dark situations. One of those small key-ring torches might be a good investment for those planning a lot of work in darkness.

The film rewind crank...
...on the left of the top plate winds the exposed film back into its cassette. When the rewind knob is pulled up the coupling fork in the cassette chamber lifts up and enables you to insert a new film. It does not open the back cover. For this you need...

The back cover latch...
...on the left side near the base of the camera (as you hold it). Push this downwards; the camera back swings open and the frame counter indicates S, two positions before 0. When the film has been loaded, operate the film advance lever two or three times to wind the film onto the take-up spool. The frame counter moves from S to 0.

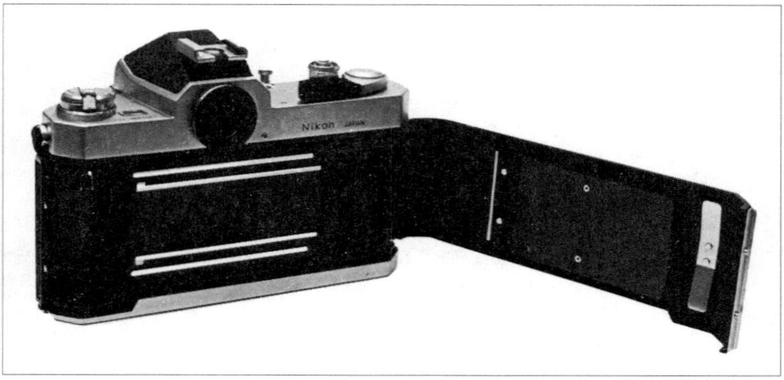

The film guide tracks of the Nikkormat FT2 are long and help to hold the film in the required flat position. The back cover cannot be exchanged - data imprint remains the prerogative of professionals and scientists.

The lens lock release button...
...to the left of the lens bayonet serves to lock the lens exactly in position for the aperture to function properly. To release the lens, just press this button and twist off. If necessary you might need to change the shutter speed - not because it has anything to do with the lens

but because the shutter speed lever covers the lens lock release button when set to $^1/_4$, $^1/_8$ or $^1/_{15}$ sec! Above this button is...

The maximum aperture reminder...
...which covers f/1.2, f/2.8 and f/5.6.

The shutter speed lever...
...simplifying the operation of the shutter speed ring also has another function. There is a little button which when pressed can be used to enter the film speed. The range covers ISO 12/12° to ISO 1600/33° which should be enough for the requirements of most photographers and subjects. Although there are faster films available they are used only rarely. The chosen film speed must be within the brackets on the scale.

The tripod socket...
...in the base of the camera body is not an unnecessary extra. Although heavy but sturdy tripods are seldom taken on journeys, small tripods are light enough to be carried around.

The battery chamber cover...
...on the Nikkormat FT2 is slotted and can be opened by inserting a coin. The battery is a 1.5V silver oxide cell which can last for years. If changed once a year there should be no danger of power loss at an inappropriate moment.

The viewfinder...
...is the information centre for the correct exposure - but it is even more important for the composition of the picture and focusing. The viewfinder of the Nikkormat FT2 shows a little less than the 24x36mm frame. This is quite annoying when suddenly objects appear on the print or slide you could not see at the time of exposure. On the other hand a part of the picture will be covered

by the slide frame or cut off from the print anyway.

In the centre of the focusing screen there are two focusing aids - a horizontal split-image rangefinder and a microprism ring surrounding it. When the subject is incorrectly focused the split-image finder cuts through the image with an offset line and the microprism starts to flicker. Rotate the focusing ring on the lens until the line is straight and the image in the microprism is sharp. Both aids cannot be used equally well in all situations, but one of them is always usable. Difficulties arise with slow lenses - f/5.6 and less. The slow speed causes the focusing aids to darken partially or even completely. You can avoid this somewhat by looking absolutely straight into the centre of the viewfinder.

Nikkormat FT3 - a close relation

In 1977 the Nikon bayonets were converted to the AI type fitting. The new lenses still featured the typical meter coupling prong which enabled them to be used with older Nikon cameras such as the FT2. For AI generation cameras this fork was no longer required, though. The largest opening is transmitted to the exposure meter automatically when attaching the lens.

One of the AI generation cameras is the Nikkormat FT3. But despite the new name this camera only differed from the FT2 by the new AI bayonet, all the other technical details remained the same. The name FT2-AI would possibly have been clearer but this is a matter of opinion.

The FT3 can also be used with the older automatic Nikkor lenses although exposure metering is only possible at working aperture. Older lenses with open aperture metering for the Nikkormat FT3 (like other cameras with AI connection) can be fitted with an AI connection by a Nikon dealer.

Nikon FM - Smaller, Lighter, More Convenient

In 1977 the Olympus OM-1 had been in production for some 5 years and it proved how small a 35mm SLR camera could be. Nikon, as always a little sceptical where new trends and their conversion into technology are concerned, only then started to react with a new series of cameras headed by the Nikon FM. Its successor, the FM2, is still on the market today.

The Nikon bayonet was also changed in 1977 and the Nikon FM was designed for the new AI bayonet.

The Nikon FM, compared to the Olympus OM-1 or Pentax MX, is still a fairly large camera, although noticeably smaller than previous Nikon SLR cameras. It is a comfortable camera to hold, especially when the motor drive MD-12 designed for this camera is attached.

Exposure Metering - new cells, old weighting

For the first time the Nikon FM used gallium instead of cadmium sulphide or silicon for the metering sensor. Galium is a material that enables the exposure meter to react quickly even in low light. It is possible to meter different subject parts in rapid succession without one metering result affecting the other. Although this is not a grave problem with other metering cells, either, it does give you peace of mind.

Metering in rapid succession is not such a hypothetical idea as it might at first seem. Some high-contrast subjects with noticeable differences in the brightness

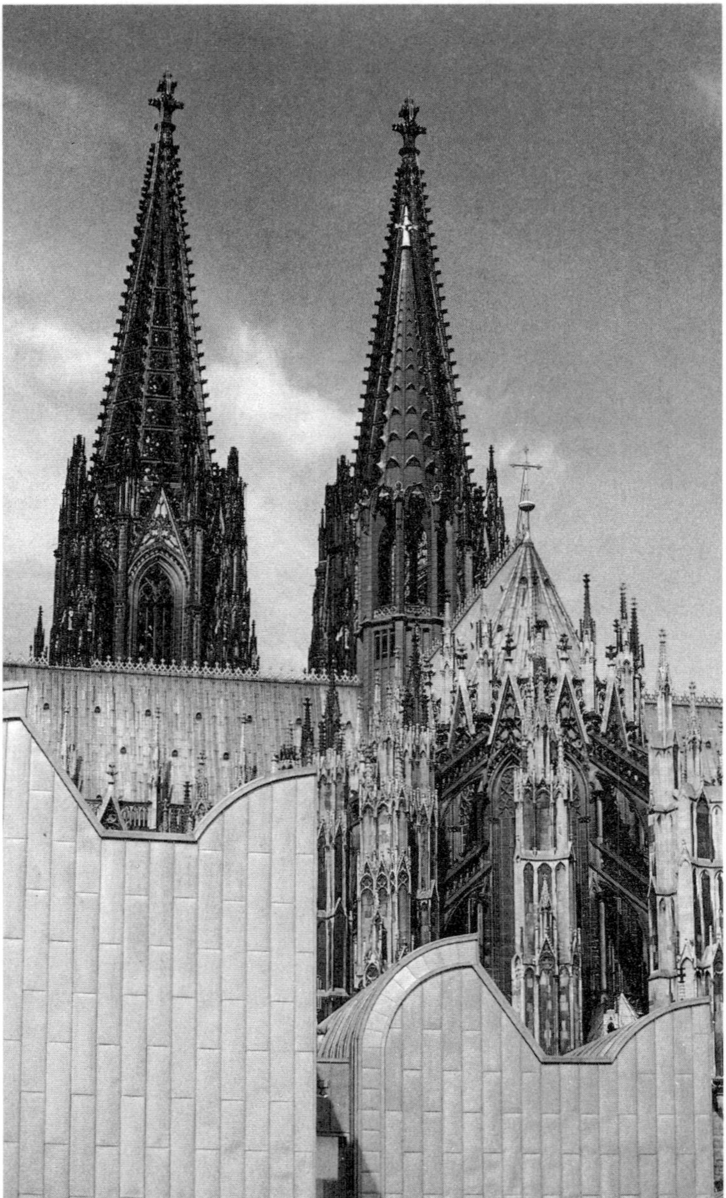

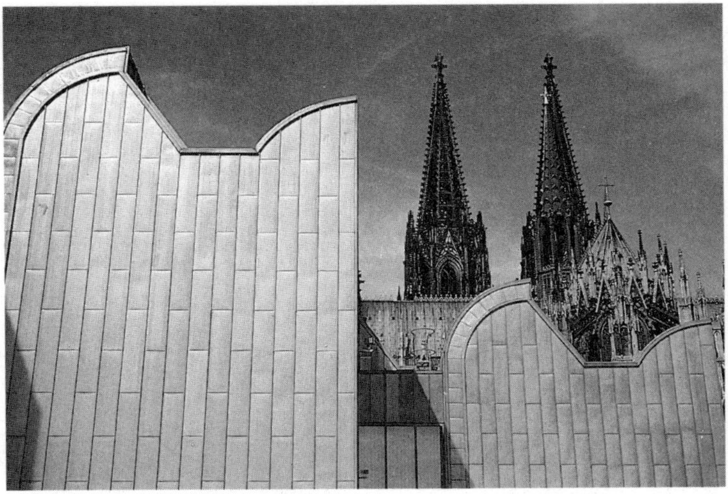

The cathedral is a standard subject for every visitor to Cologne. A short walk around·the monument yields new views - for example the contrast between the Gothic church and the modern Wallraf-Richartz Museum. If you take the time, you can take many different shots of this new subject. A change of focal length and shooting position interprets the interaction between two buildings completely differently. In one shot the Middle Age dominates (longer shooting distance, medium focal length), in the other the modern building pushes the Cathedral into the background. Zoom lenses make it easy to choose the exact image section. Even without a tripod, a motor drive allows the image section to be retained precisely while using different apetures (and different depths of field).

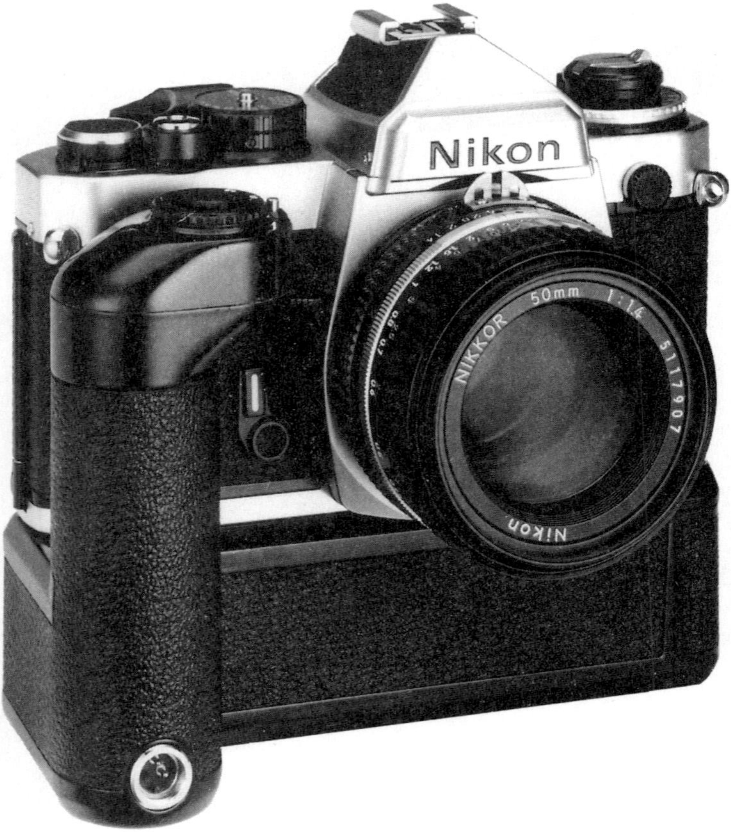

A new Nikon era starts with the Nikon FM. The old type bayonet was replaced by the AI bayonet. However, the change only affected the exposure metering system - the old lenses still fitted on the new cameras. The new lenses also continued to be fitted with the familiar meter coupling prong so that they could be used with the old cameras. Together with the MD-11 motor drive the Nikon FM forms a handy photographic unit.

between highlights and shadows could overtax the film material. If you determine the amount of contrast when metering you can control the exposure in such a way that the most important parts are exposed correctly and either the highlights or the shadows are still well rendered.

To meter several subject parts separately is no problem with the Nikon FM. The metering system is the same as that of other Nikon SLR cameras - centre weighted integrating. The 12mm diameter circle in the centre of the viewfinder accounts for 60% and the surrounding area 40% of the metering result. Especially when longer focal lengths are used for metering rather than for the actual picture the main subject can be metered very easily. If the subject itself is not suitable for metering because it is too light or too dark the central metering circle can be used to meter a substitute subject which will ensure correct exposure.

Correct exposure is not always the best exposure in all cases. Sometimes slight under or overexposure gives a more interesting picture. But it is easy with the Nikon FM to achieve the kind of exposure you have planned.

Exposure Control - follow the signals

The exposure meter - whether powered by gallium cells or not - determines a suitable exposure value for the given film speed and subject brightness.

As the Nikon FM is designed for manual exposure control it is up to you to select the shutter speed/ aperture combination from the right exposure value. The camera just points the way for you and also indicates when you deviate from it.

On the right-hand side of the viewfinder image a narrow strip extends slightly into the image area showing the symbols "+", "o" and "-". To the right of each symbol is a red LED. When the exposure meter is switched on by pulling the film advance lever away from the camera body, one or two of these LEDs light up. The LED next to the + lights up when the shutter speed and aperture setting will lead to overexposure by more than 1 stop. The LEDs next to the + and 0 indicate overexposure by $^1/_5$ to 1 stop. The LEDs next to the 0 and the - indicate underexposure by $^1/_5$ to 1 stop, the LED next to the - indicates underexposure by more than 1 stop. The LED next to the 0 indicates correct exposure.

In addition to this display there are signals for aperture, which is read directly off the AI lens via optics, and the shutter speed.

Depending on whether you want a specific depth of field or whether you want to freeze or blur movement you can select an aperture or shutter speed and then change the other factor until the LED indicates 0.

The available aperture range is determined by the lens. The shutter speed range extends from 1 to $^1/_{1000}$ sec plus the B setting where the shutter remains open until the shutter release button is released. A cable release is very useful for this.

The information also enables you to react quickly to difficult lighting conditions.

---

llustrations opposite:
Two different effects of backlighting. The autumn colours of the leaf glow because light shines through the leaf. However, the branches and part of a forest in front of a light background appear dark and lifeless.

Illustration on page 88:
When tall subjects are to be photographed, wide-angle lenses used at close range tend to produce converging lines. This can be avoided by taking the photograph from a longer distance with a longer focal length lens, provided there is sufficient space in front of the subject.

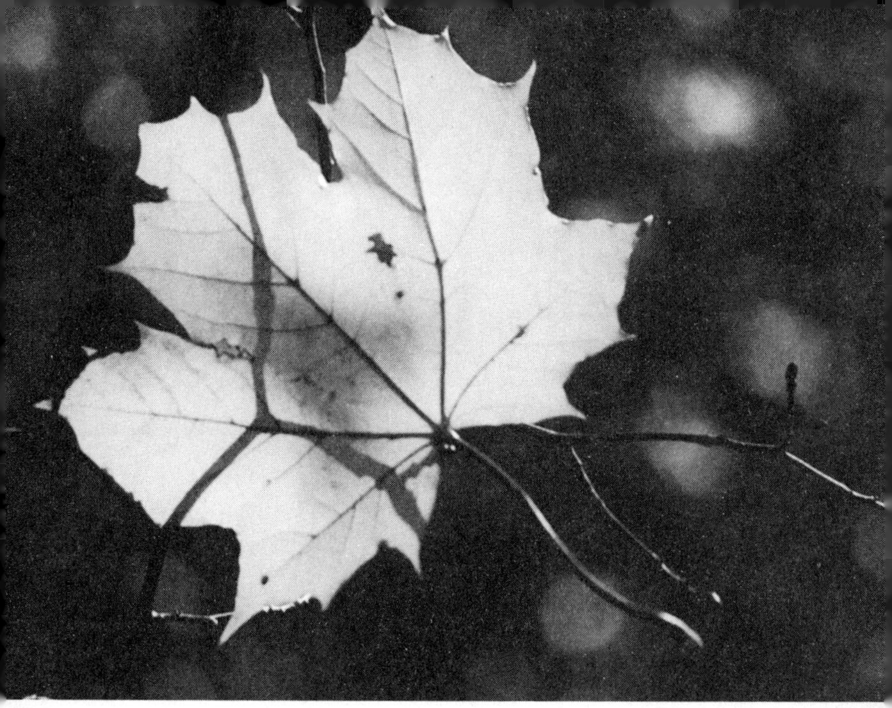

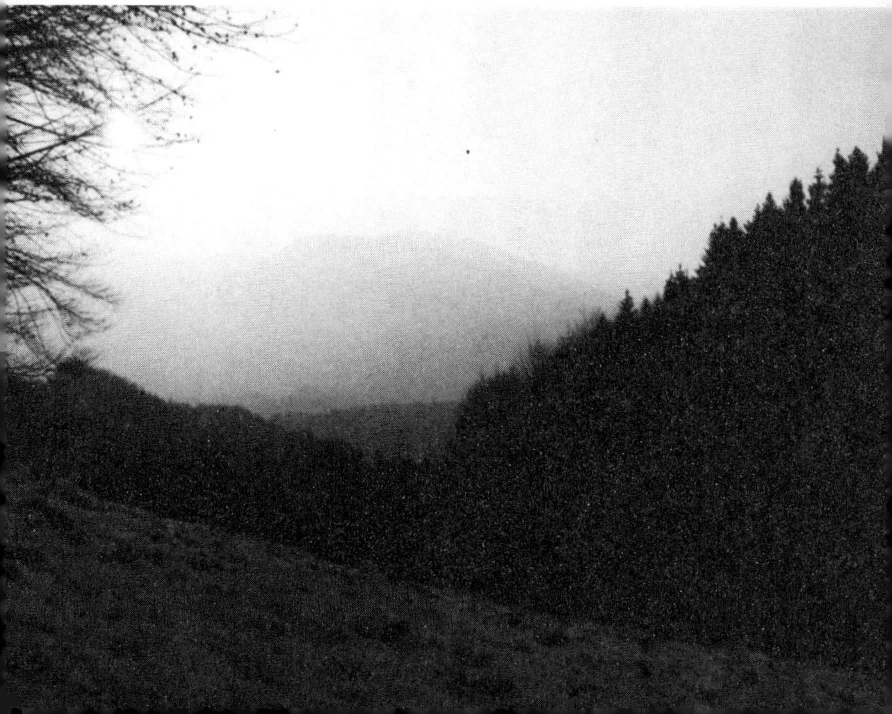

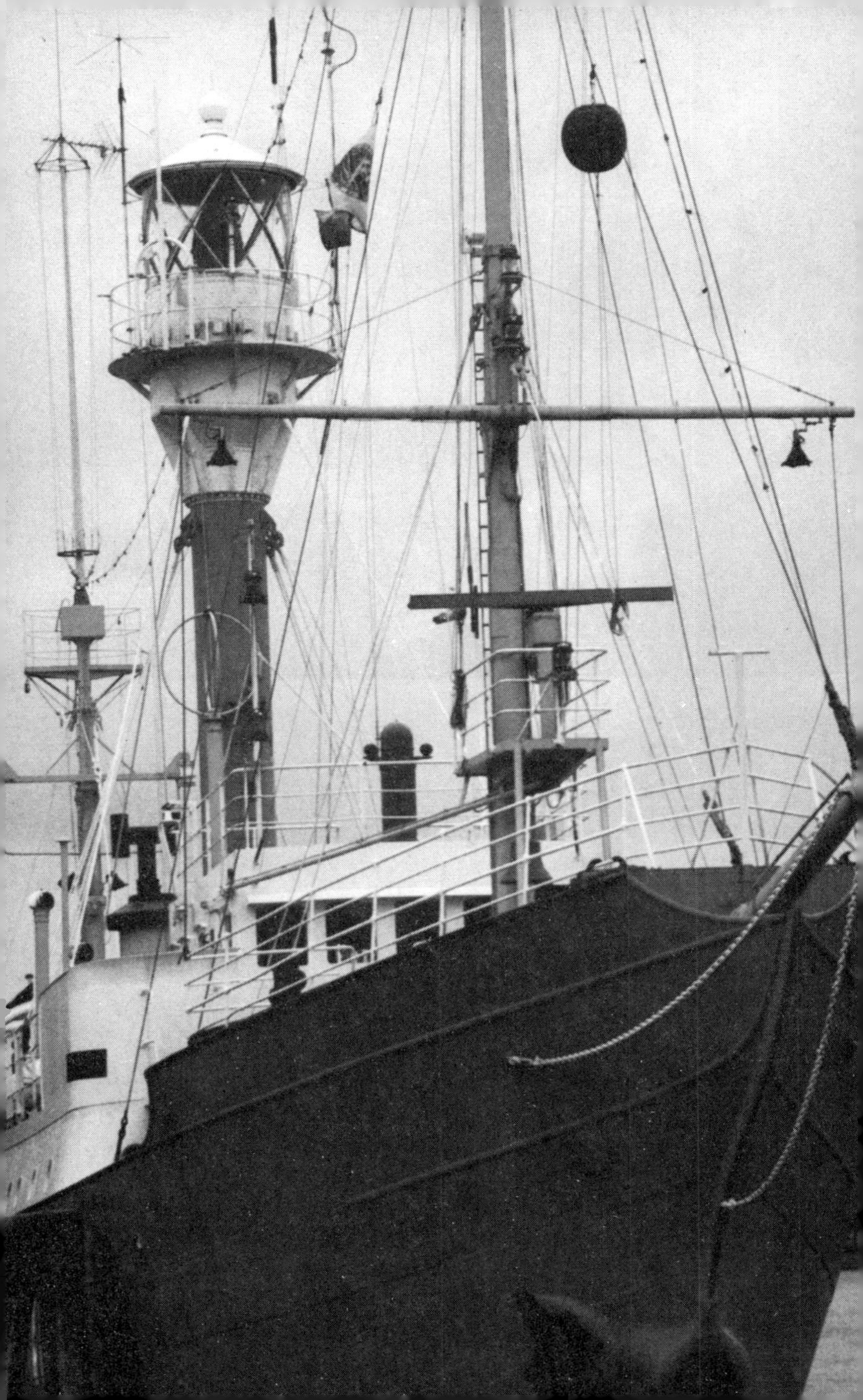

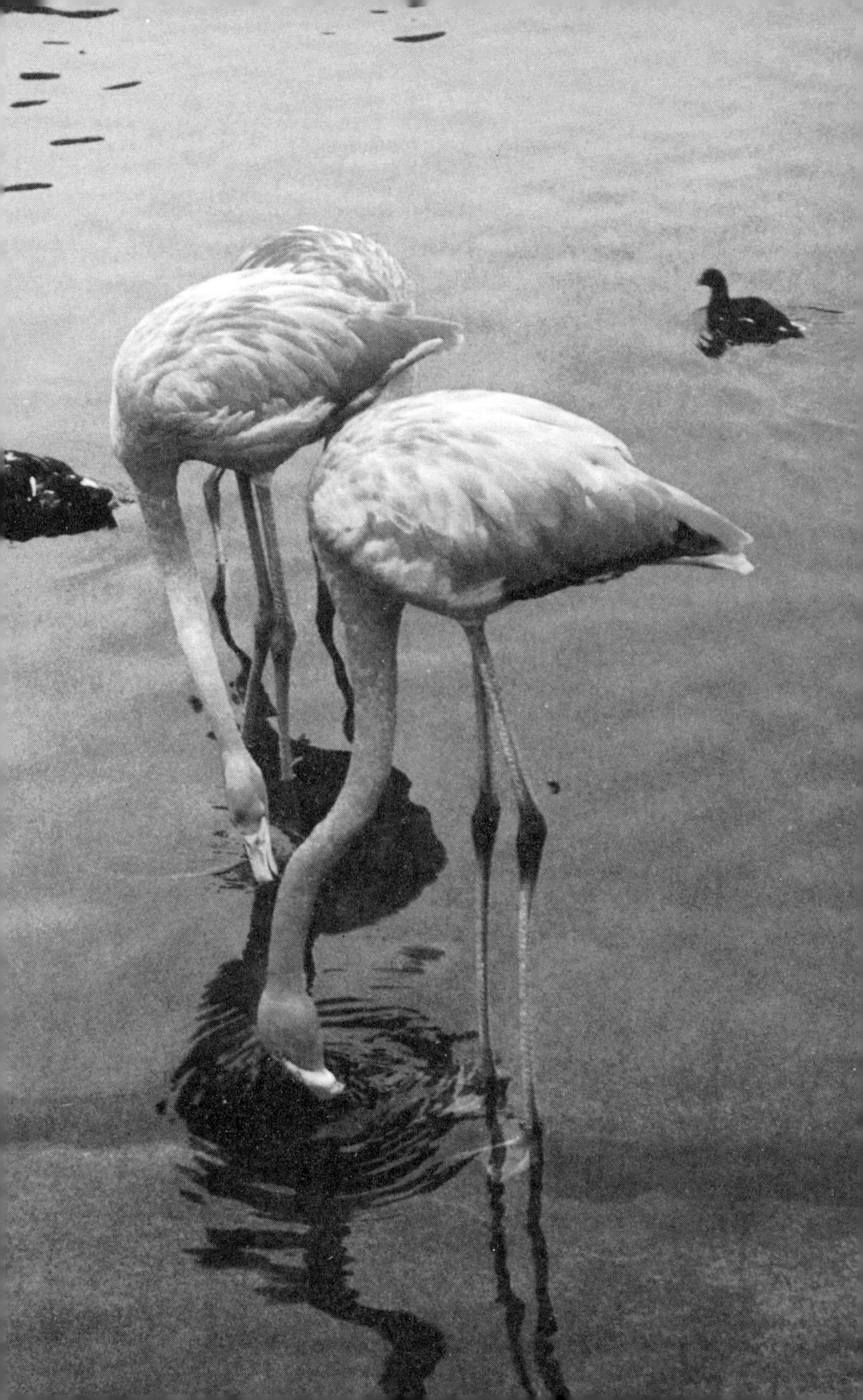

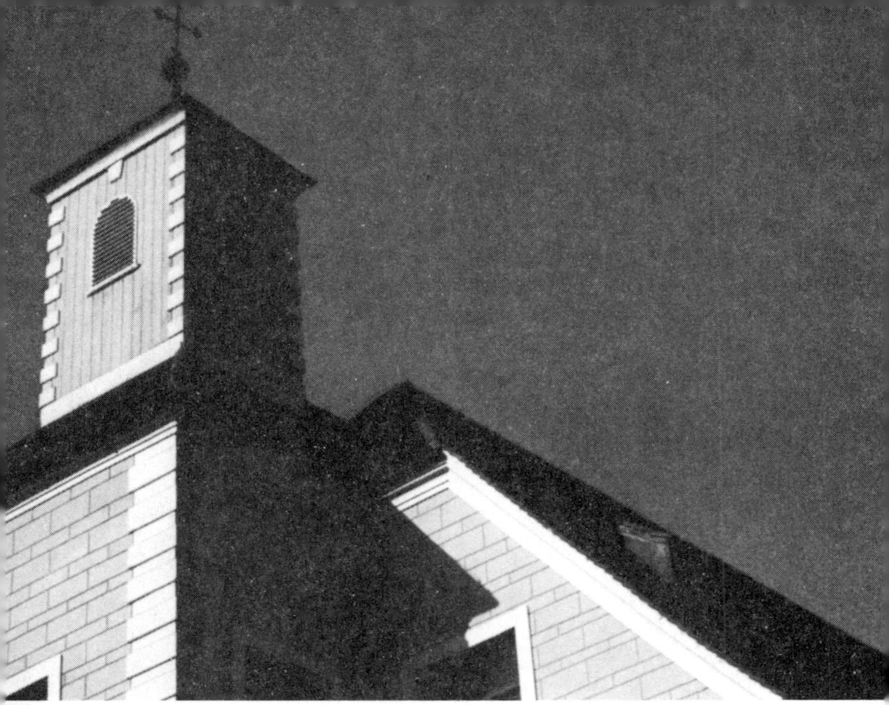

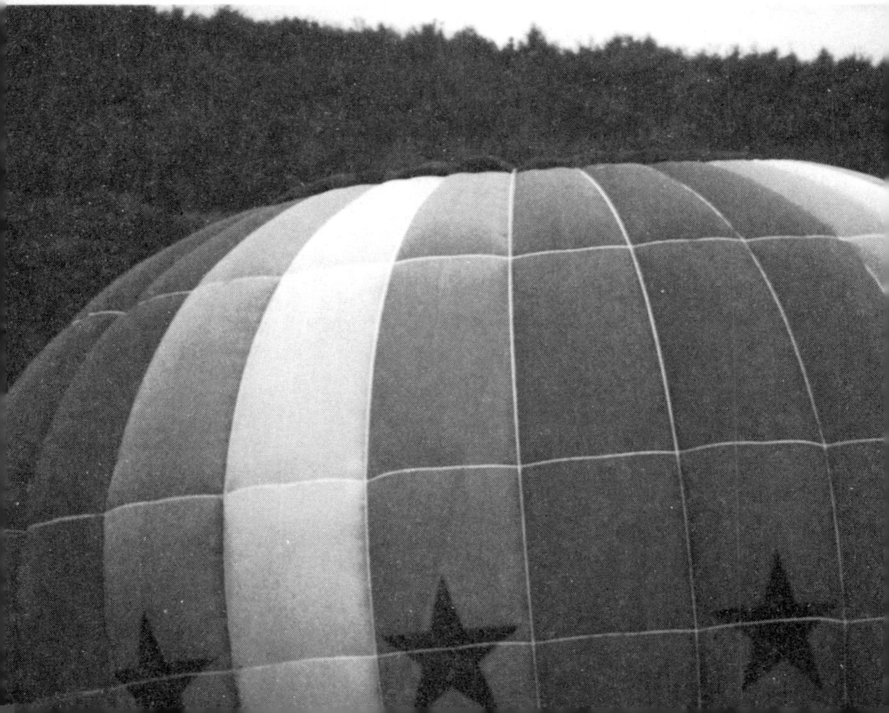

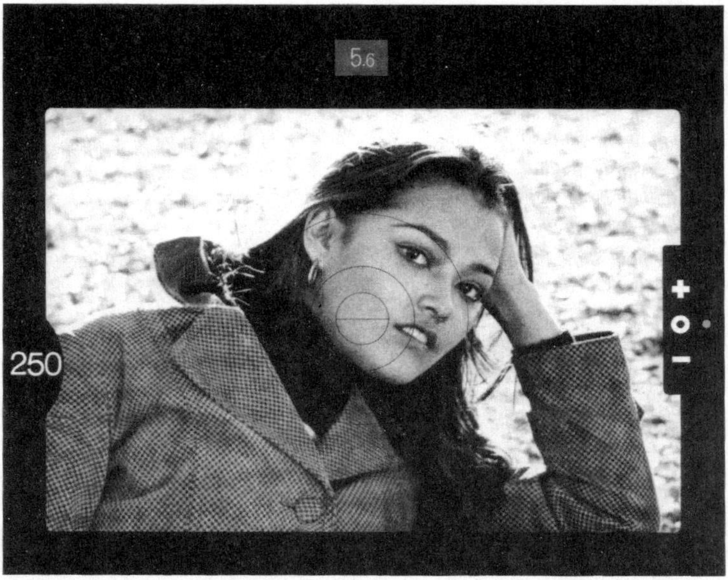

The viewfinder gives the photographer all the important data. But it is hard to understand why we have to look at three sides of the viewfinder image in order to get an overview. The shutter speed is shown on the left, the aperture at the top, and on the right the exposure meter 'traffic light'.

Illustration on page 89:
The camera often stays at home because the weather isn't good enough. But an overcast sky does have its advantages in photography. The colours appear delicate, almost as pastels, which is particularly flattering for these flamingoes!

Illustration opposite:
You don't always have to have the whole subject in the frame - striking details are always worth a shot. Zoom lenses are a great help in such situations because the image section can be selected without a change in the shooting position, which always means a change of perspective.

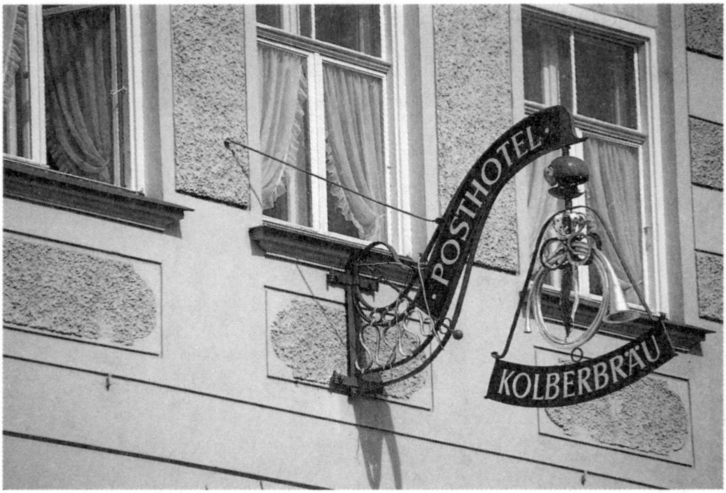

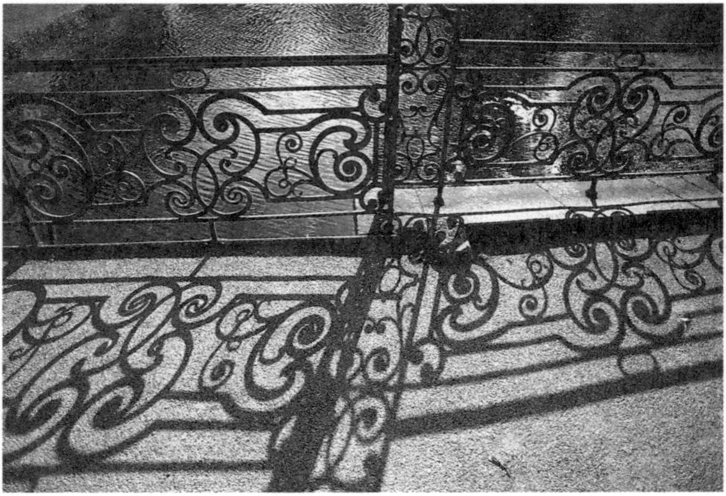

With a low-contrast subject (top), exposure metering can take place at the centre of the image and the result will be right every time. But when the shot is dominated by stronger contrasts (bottom), take advantage of the strong centre-weighting and measure the exposure at the most suitable point - in this case the fairly neutral foreground - by directing the centre circle in the viewfinder on it.

Working Aperture Metering - rarely used but still possible

The Nikon lens mounting remained on the whole unchanged with the introduction of lenses with an AI bayonet. All Nikkors on the market since the arrival of the Nikon F can also be used on the Nikon FM and all Nikon cameras with AI bayonet. These mountings no longer feature the typical coupling pin which was taken up by the meter coupling prong on the aperture control ring of the lens and which informed the camera of the maximum aperture of the lens. Instead the maximum aperture of the AI lenses is automatically transferred to the camera by a cam.

This all means that Nikkors without AI characteristics cannot be used with open aperture metering as the camera does not know the largest aperture. Although it is possible to modify older auto Nikkors, these lenses can be used on the Nikon FM anyway. In order to attach the lens to the camera the metering coupling lever release button in the camera bayonet to the right of the cam must be pressed and the meter coupling lever, which is caught by the cam of AI lenses, folded upwards.

The exposure meter is switched on as usual. First determine the framing and then press the depth of field preview lever. The lens aperture closes to the value preset on the aperture ring. Afterwards the exposure can be set correctly with the appropriate shutter speed/aperture combination. Exposure control via the shutter speed is a little tricky as shutter speed dial and depth of field preview lever are both situated on the right side of the camera. Hold the camera in your right hand, press the depth of field preview lever with your right middle finger and reach over the viewfinder prism with your left hand to operate the shutter speed dial. Once the LED in the viewfinder display signals 0 for correct exposure the depth of field preview lever can be released and the shutter release pressed.

The exposure is also controlled like this with older lenses without meter coupling prong but with auto iris.

Exposure control with lenses without auto iris (e.g. PC Nikkors) or with lenses and accessories that do not transfer any aperture function (e.g. bellows, extension rings or focusing aids) require no depth of field preview lever as the alteration of the aperture ring is directly transferred to the iris in the lens.

Backlighting - interesting but not that easy

Although the exposure meter of the Nikon FM is very good it can be overtaxed by difficult situations such as back lighting. The problem lies in the fact that the actual subject is in front of the bright background which causes the exposure meter to give a high exposure value for the shutter speed/aperture combination. The result is that the background is normally slightly overexposed (it is adapted to the grey value of the normal subject) and the main subject is underexposed.

There are two possible solutions to this problem. The right amount of longer exposure will be too much for the background but the main subject will be correctly exposed. This plus compensation can easily be achieved with the Nikon FM. First set shutter speed and aperture so that the LED indicates 0 and then open the aperture by 1 to $1^1/_2$ stops. The extent of the compensation can be calculated more precisely by metering the main subject (close-up metering, decreasing the metering angle by using a longer focal length).

Another way to achieve satisfactory backlit pictures is to slightly underexpose whereby the background - perhaps the blue sky with white clouds above a windmill - appears in rich colours and the foreground appears as a silhouette. For minus compensation calculate the exposure from the bright background and close the aperture by a half or a whole stop.

This option to get the most out of backlit situations is based on the manipulation of speed and aperture, i.e. they can be achieved without additional means. Apart from this there is, of course, yet another way to adapt main subject and back lighting to each other. This is the method of lightening the subject by adding more light to the front.

You can utilize the existing light by using some reflective material such as white card, fabric or polystyrene. The advantage of this method is that the light will be soft. The disadvantage is that you need to carry a reflecting surface with you and also someone to hold the reflector if you are not opting for one of the professional reflectors which are equipped with a tripod. Another method to lighten the subject is a flash. First meter the background where the centre weighted integrated metering is of help and set the aperture according to the sync speed ($^1/_{125}$ sec on the Nikon FM). If the background is very bright - snow, for example - open the aperture by a stop. This ensures that the background is correctly exposed. Adopt the selected aperture as the flash aperture and set it on the computer flash unit. If the flash unit happens not to feature this aperture the matter becomes a little more complicated, but this also can be remedied. Suppose that the right aperture is f/5.6 but the flash only has computer apertures f/4 and f/8. In this case set f/8 on the camera's aperture ring and on the flash. To ensure that the background remains correctly exposed decrease the shutter speed from $^1/_{125}$ to $^1/_{60}$ sec. This will not affect the flash exposure despite the fact that $^1/_{125}$ sec is given as the sync speed. This only means that the flash cannot be used for faster speeds whereas all speeds slower than $^1/_{125}$ sec can be used with the flash. The shutter speed/aperture combination of $^1/_{60}$ sec and f/8 which allows the same amount of light to reach the film as $^1/_{125}$ sec and f/5.6 will take care of the background and the computer flash ensures that the main subject is correctly exposed at f/8.

Film Speeds - great range for small compensations

The film speed range of the Nikon FM is rather extensive and runs from ISO 12/12° to ISO 3200/36°.

This enables you to compensate for slower films such as Kodachrome 25. On the other hand modern high speed films can also be utilized and even ISO 1600 corrected towards minus.

Exposure compensation affecting only a few pictures is a simple matter with the Nikon FM. Set the correct exposure and open or close the aperture by the desired value. Compensation via the film speeds is unsuitable here. This should be used when the situation demands exposure compensation - such as snow where a longer exposure by $^2/_3$ or 1 stop ensures that the beautiful whiteness does not appear as a slushy grey. Set the film

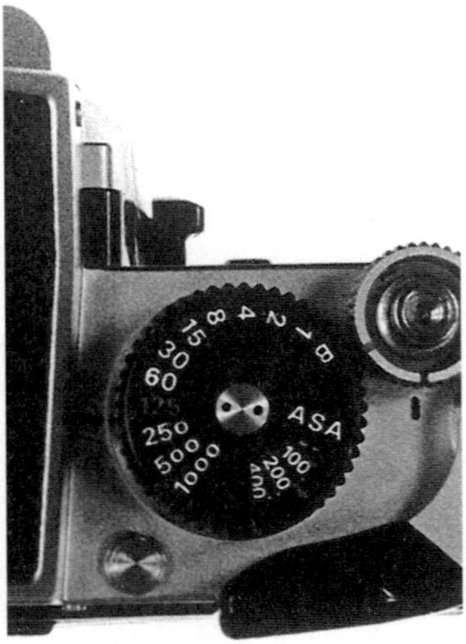

The shutter speed dial of the Nikon FM is also used to set the film speed. The shutter release button can be locked to avoid the possibility of accidental exposures.

speed two or three steps lower than required as a result of the given film speed, i.e. for an Ektachrome 100 set a film speed of ISO 64/19° or ISO 50/18°. Afterwards meter the exposure for the different subjects as usual and even if this results in different shutter speed/aperture combinations each picture will be overexposed by $^2/_3$ to 1 stop. Remember to reset the film speed to the correct value when compensation is no longer needed.

Multiple Exposures - simple but tricky

There is a good reason for modern cameras to feature a multiple exposure facility. When two separate operations were required to wind on the film and cock the shutter it often happened that after cocking the shutter the photographer forgot to wind on the film, resulting in a double exposure of the same frame and thus two spoilt pictures. This cannot happen with the Nikon FM as cocking the shutter and film wind are coupled together, i.e. exposure is only possible when an unexposed frame lies in the film plane.

As convenient as such a safety feature is for most situations it can be irritating at other times. Deliberate double exposures can make a very interesting picture.

The Nikon FM is equipped with a special button for double or multiple exposures. This is located to the left behind the shutter speed dial. After each shot first push it to the left and then operate the film advance lever in order to cock the shutter and expose the frame twice. In principle this is no different to using the rewind release button, but because the film is not completely released - it cannot be rewound once the multiple exposure button has been pressed - it remains static in the camera while the shutter is cocked.

Good double or multiple exposures require an accurate eye. The different parts of the individual subjects must match. If some time passes between the individual exposures a brief diagram of the scene might be useful. Another point to take into account in connection with multiple exposures is the light.

When several frame-filling subjects are joined together the light reaching the film adds up. If each shot is exposed according to the meter calculations the result will be clearly overexposed. In this case the exposure of individual shots must be reduced. Halve the exposure in the case of double exposures (aperture closed by 1 stop or shutter speed faster by one setting). In the case of multiple exposures the correction depends on the number of shots you wish to make. For three shots close the aperture by $1^1/_2$ stops, for four shots by 2 stops. These are only guidelines which could vary according to the situation.

The case is different, though, when you want to make a picture of three or four objects on a black background which must not overlap each other. Meter the exposure from the main subject and correct only slightly towards minus, so that the black background remains as such.

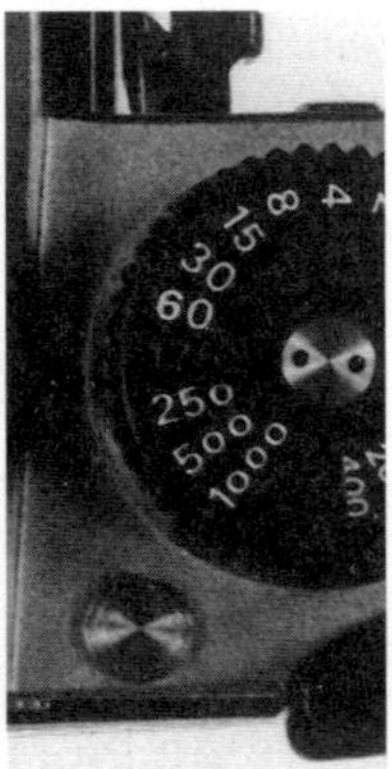

Visible to the left behind the shutter speed dial is the button which can be used to release the film winding mechanism in order to make multiple exposures.

Features - practical and well thought out

The operating features on the compact Nikon FM are arranged clearly and logically. Contrary to the FT models (FT, FTN, FT2 and FT3) the...

Shutter speed dial...
...is again in the same position we know from many other cameras - to the left of the viewfinder prism. Shutter speeds from 1 to $^1/_{1000}$ sec are represented in fractions of a second, e.g. 125 stands for $^1/_{125}$. This speed is marked in red as it represents the fastest sync speed at which a flash can be used. The shutter speed dial also serves as the...

Film speed index...
For this function lift the knurled ring against a slight resistance and turn it. The film speeds will appear in a small window in the top of the dial. Indicated are the ASA values which are the first figures of the ISO value.

The shutter release button...
...to the right of the shutter speed dial has two sockets for the connection of cable releases. One of the threads

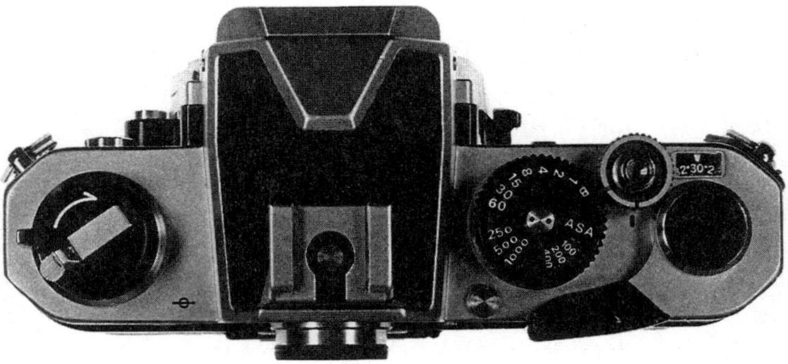

The Nikon FM may be smaller than earlier generations of Nikon cameras, but it handles well, and the operating controls can be reached comfortably.

is incorporated into the release button to accommodate the most commonly-used type of cable release. The outer thread is designed for a variant of the cable release known as a "Leica bell". The shutter remains locked as long as the film advance lever is in the folded position.

The shutter release lock/mode selector...
...surrounding the shutter release is required when a motor drive is attached. The ring is set to the red index for motor drive operation and to the black one for normal working.

The frame counter...
...is found to the right of the shutter release. It forward counts the exposed frames and resets to "0" automatically when the camera back is opened.

The film advance lever...
...on the top right of the camera also serves as the main switch for activating the exposure meter, when pulled away from the camera body just enough to uncover a red dot.

The multi exposure button...
...to the left behind the shutter speed dial is rather insignificant and if you make double or multiple exposures only infrequently you can easily forget the function of this button.

The accessory shoe...
...on top of the viewfinder prism is designed to accept a hot contact for the cableless connection of flash units. This shoe accepts several other kinds of accessories as well such as a small spirit level to ensure vertical lines in architectural photography.

The accessory shoe is permanently fixed on the roof of the viewfinder prism. The rewind crank on the far left is important even when the MD-11 or MD-12 motor drive is used - they only transport the film in a forward direction.

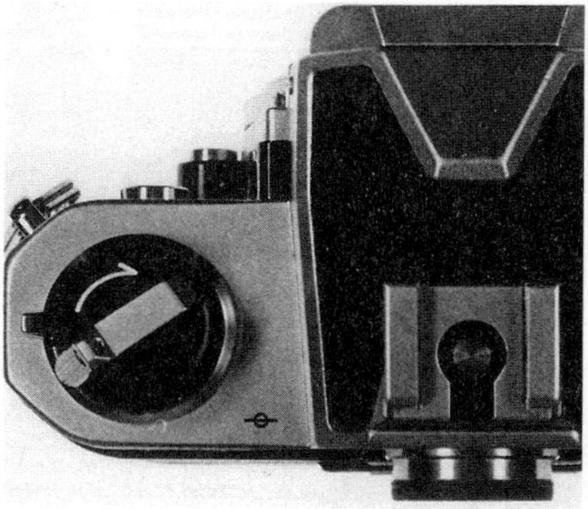

The film rewind crank...

...to the left of the camera top is primarily used to wind the film back into its cassette, after pressing the film rewind on the base plate. It also has other functions such as checking whether there is a film in the camera. When carefully turned and no resistance is noticeable after one or two turns you can be sure the camera is empty or that the film is not loaded correctly. When its adjacent lock is turned anticlockwise, this allows the rewind knob to be pulled up to open the camera back.

The sync terminal...

...accepts cables of flash units without hot shoe or when the flash is to be used away from the camera. There are several reasons for this. Light coming from the side is more flattering to the subject than light coming straight from the front. Indirect flash light is softer than direct flash light. When the distance between lens and flash reflector increases the danger of "red eye" effect (effect of light being bounced off the retinas in the eyes) is reduced.

The lens release button...
...has to be pressed before a lens can be lifted out of the mounting flange. It is located on the right front of the camera.

The depth of field preview...
...on the left front of the camera is used when the exposure for certain lenses is metered at working aperture, but this is not its main function. The aperture clearly influences the extent of depth of field which also depends on the focal length and the subject distance. This lever allows the aperture to be closed to the required value before the shot is made and the effect of sharpness and blur of the subject to be judged. Open aperture metering always shows the smallest depth of field possible with a particular lens.

The self-timer lever...
...is also located on the left front of the camera. It has to be pressed downwards to activate the delay function. The further down the lever is pressed the longer the delay before shutter release. The longest delay is about 14 sec. If you change your mind while the sequence is running just return the lever to its starting position and shoot as normal.

It can be used to avoid camera shake which occurs with slow shutter speeds. When the self-timer is used the mirror springs up immediately upon pressing the shutter release button and any vibration ceases before the shutter is actually released. This function is especially valuable in connection with long lenses or in macrophotography.

The battery compartment...
...in the camera base accepts two 1.5V button cells. Loading the batteries is easy because the compartment cover is equipped with a clamp on the inside holding

the batteries securely. Ensure that the batteries are inserted correctly.

The tripod socket...
...is located underneath the optical axis of the lens and has a 1/4" thread.

The rewind release button...
...is used to uncouple the winding mechanism so that the take-up spool can revolve backwards for the film to return to its cassette.

The motor drive connections...
...in the camera base allow motor drive MD-12 to be connected to the camera.

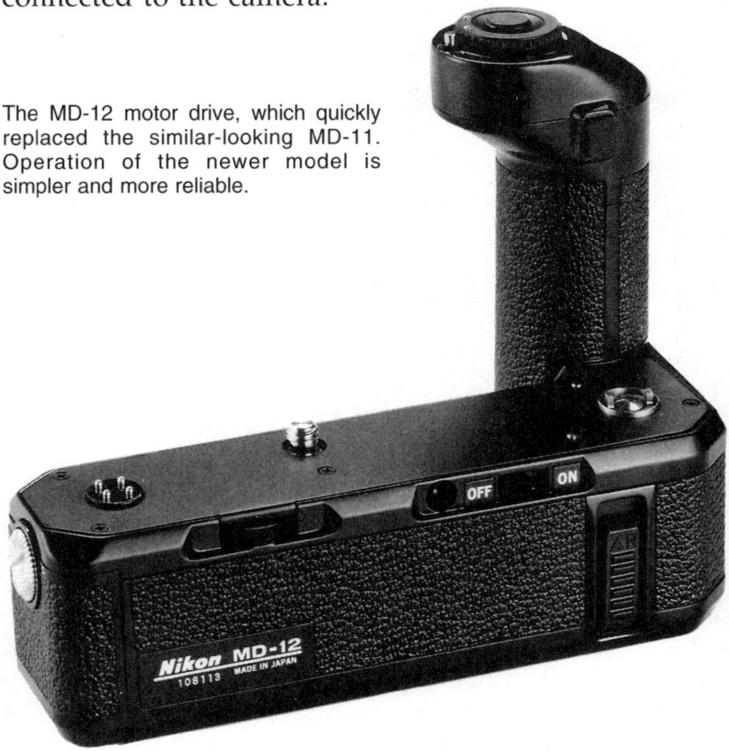

The MD-12 motor drive, which quickly replaced the similar-looking MD-11. Operation of the newer model is simpler and more reliable.

Nikon FE2 - Automatically to the Top

After the Nikon FM in 1977and its sister model FE with shutter priority in 1978, Nikon concentrated on newcomers to photography with the Nikon EM and the Nikon FG, and also the professionals with variations of the Nikon F3. The next big impact was made with the FM2, the first camera featuring $^1/_{4000}$ sec as the fastest shutter speed. And just as a year had to pass between the introduction of the FM and the appearance of the FE we had to wait a year before we were offered the FE2 in 1983.

Compact Nikons took over, the body of the Nikon FM was also used for the FE, the FM2 and then for the FE2. It is extremely comfortable to hold, not too bulky but big enough for larger hands.

Exposure Control - a very wide range

When the Nikon FE2 came on the market it was no longer a secret that automatic exposure was a good thing and not just for people who know nothing of photography.

Like the Nikkormat EL and the Nikon FE, the automatic exposure control of the FE2 is based on aperture priority. The apertures that can be preselected depend on the lens attached but the apertures that should be selected depend on the subject.

The actual part in focus is only the plane of the subject the lens is aimed at. Before and behind this the extent of depth of field depends on the focal length of the lens, the subject distance and the aperture. The rule

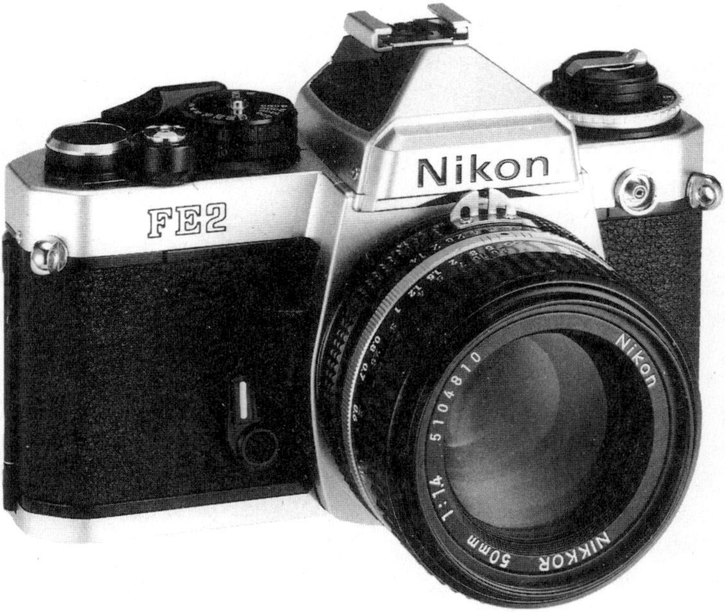

Introduced as the fastest SLR camera in the world, the Nikon FE2 offers a fastest shutter speed of 1/4000 and an X-sync speed of 1/250s. The FE2 is fitted with an AI bayonet and the meter coupling prong of an attached lens has no use on this camera.

is, the shorter the focal length the greater the depth of field, as long as aperture and focusing distance are constant. That means that at f/8 and a focusing distance of 5m a wide-angle lens will show a greater depth of field than a telephoto.

The greater the distance the bigger the depth of field - as long as focal length and aperture are constant, i.e. of two 50mm lenses both set to f/5.6 the one further away from the subject will give the greater depth of field.

The smaller the aperture (i.e. the higher the f/ number) the greater the depth of field when distance and focal length are constant. That means that of two 50mm lenses both focused to a distance of 10m the lens whose aperture is smaller will have the greater depth of field.

Aperture priority allows you to use sharpness and blur to compose the subject to the greatest effect.

Panoramic views of landscapes or interiors are best photographed with a wide-angle lens and as small an aperture as possible to achieve sharpness from the front right to the back.

If you want to separate your subject from the surroundings, e.g. portraits or a group of trees from a landscape, choose a wide open aperture which will give you a small depth of field. As lenses with longer focal lengths - from 85mm onwards - are often used in these cases the separation of sharp subject and blurred background becomes easier.

Aperture priority almost always selects a suitable shutter speed, but it is prudent to know a little about automatic exposure, especially when a large depth of field is required. Small apertures occasionally demand very slow shutter speeds, perhaps a landscape at dusk

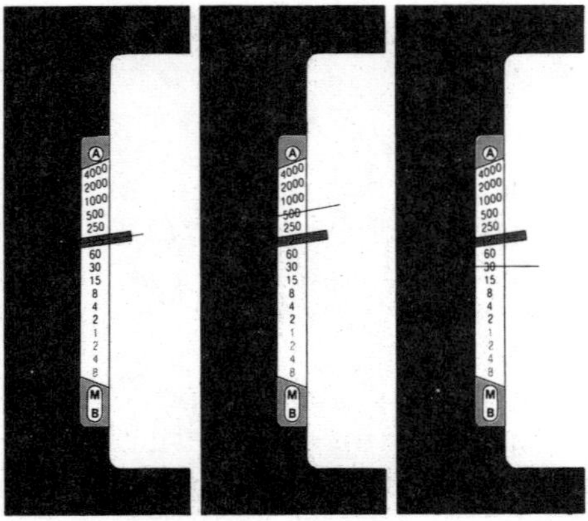

Correct exposure   Overexposure   Underexposure

The indication on the left-hand side of the viewfinder image provides information about the operating mode and automatically-selected shutter speed; it also warns of over- or underexposure when the camera is used in automatic exposure mode. With manual metering, correct exposure is achieved when the wide pointer and the black meter needle are aligned by changing the shutter speed and/or aperture. Exposure compensation can be controlled very precisely.

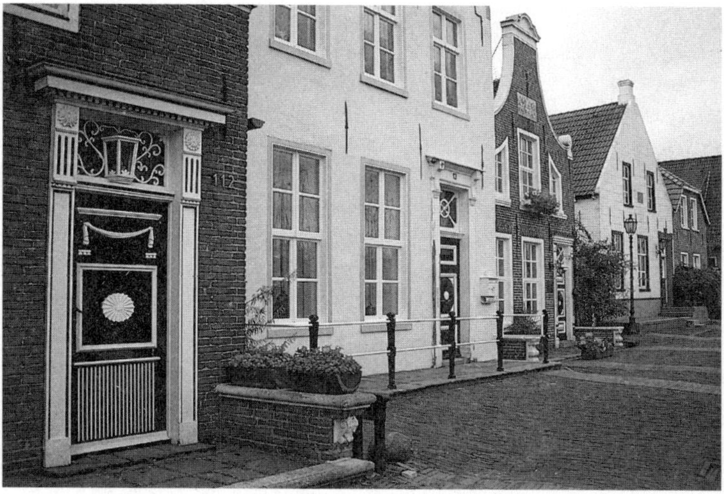

Aperture selection in aperture priority mode allows the photographer to influence the depth of field. Choosing the right aperture is easy with the help of the depth of field preview lever.

or an interior shot without flash, and slow speeds can lead to camera shake blur.

To the left of the viewfinder image is a shutter speed scale, above which can be seen an A in a red field while beneath the scale there is an M and a B, also within a red field. The upper field indicates overexposure, the lower underexposure.

In aperture priority mode a wide green pointer indicates the A while a black metering index over the scale shows the shutter speed automatically selected according to the aperture.

If the shutter speed is slower than "one divided by focal length in mm" - the hand-held limit - there is no need to worry. However, if the closed aperture requires a slower shutter speed, use a tripod. If the shutter speed is only a little slower a pocket tripod such as the Cullmann Magic II is adequate.

Nikon designed the Nikon FE2 to provide very slow shutter speeds, right up to 8 sec. If even this is too fast the FE2 warns of impending underexposure. You can either open the aperture or select a slower shutter speed via the B setting. This might be difficult, however, when a colour slide film is used as the colours could be falsified because of low intensity reciprocity failure.

For a very small depth of field a very bright ambient light may require a very fast shutter speed - especially if a high speed Ektachrome 400 is loaded. Until the introduction of the Nikon FM2 the only options were to change the film or to use a neutral density filter. The FM2 offered a fastest shutter speed of $^{1}/_{4000}$ sec and this is also available with the Nikon FE2.

It is an incredibly fast speed which naturally not only regulates the large amount of light when large apertures are used. This speed, for example, can actually freeze the movement of a flying helicopter's rotors, suspend the droplets of a water fountain in the air or stop the movement of a racing car. To achieve this you can either select an aperture that will require $^{1}/_{4000}$ sec or manually select the shutter speed of $^{1}/_{4000}$ and set the appropriate aperture.

Manual Aperture Control and Mechanically-controlled Shutter Speeds - nothing is impossible

When $^{1}/_{4000}$ sec is all you want, turn the shutter speed selector dial from the locked A position to 4000. You can see in the viewfinder that the green pointer leaves its position and points to 4000 while the black index indicates the shutter speed that is suitable for the aperture already set. By turning the aperture ring both pointers can be aligned and you get a correctly-exposed picture.

Naturally this applies not only to $^{1}/_{4000}$ sec but to all available shutter speeds as well. Manually you can select the shutter speeds in whole steps and the aperture in half stops, whereas in the automatic mode the selection of the shutter speeds is continuously variable. In both cases the shutter speed selection is done electronically and therefore needs power. Which means that without the two 1.5V batteries or a 3V lithium cell not only the exposure meter but also the shutter is inoperative.

This can be overcome, however, by using the mechanically-controlled emergency speed of $^{1}/_{250}$ sec. In order to calculate the required aperture either use a hand-held exposure meter or estimate the aperture. The B setting is independent of the batteries. But only speeds slower than 1 sec can reliably be controlled with the B setting because the exposure starts when the shutter release is pressed and finishes when the button is released. Should you envisage an occasion where you need to estimate and make do with $^{1}/_{250}$ sec use a negative film such as the Kodacolor Gold although you may prefer the fine grain of a Kodachrome 64 at other times. The negative film can accommodate errors within +/-2 exposure stops quite well. And good colour prints are preferable to badly exposed slides.

Exposure Metering - same as before

Exposure metering on the Nikon FE2 is centre weighted according to Nikon tradition and the centre of the viewfinder image is clearly defined by a circle. Again 60% of the centre and 40% of the surroundings make up the calculation of the required exposure value. However, activation of the exposure meter is not according to tradition. When the film advance lever is pulled away from the camera only the shutter release button is unlocked; the exposure meter is not switched on. This only happens when the shutter release button is lightly pressed. In order to free your hands you can

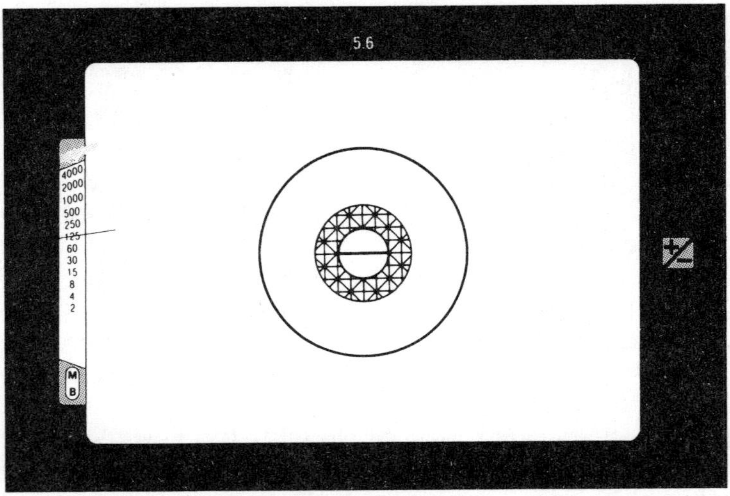

The viewfinder image area is free of exposure information. It only contains the circle (characteristic of all Nikon SLR cameras) indicating the area weighted at 60%, with the remainder at 40%, during metering. The aperture is shown above the viewfinder image, selected compensation factors on the right.

let go of the shutter button as the exposure meter remains activated for 16sec afterwards. But the reaction time of the camera's automatic control is quite fast - only moving the camera a fraction causes the metering index to show a different shutter speed. In order to still expose the picture correctly the Nikon FE2 is equipped with a memory lock.

If converging lines can't be avoided, they should be used purposefully to emphasise the height of the building. This shot of the Eiffel Tower was taken not from the base of the tower, but from the bank of the Seine which is at an even lower level. The trees and lampposts can give an idea of comparative size and also emphasise the height of the iron structure.

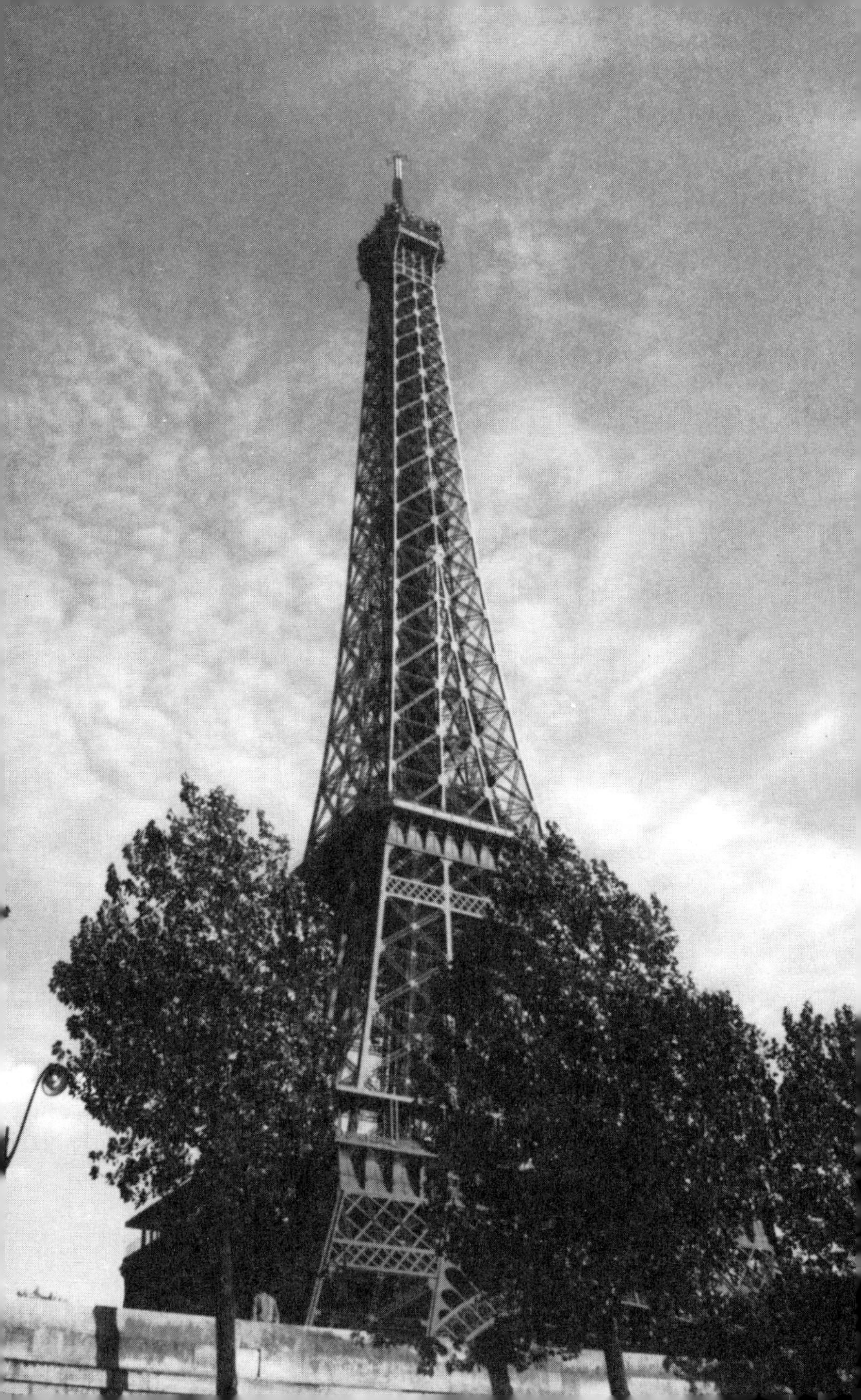

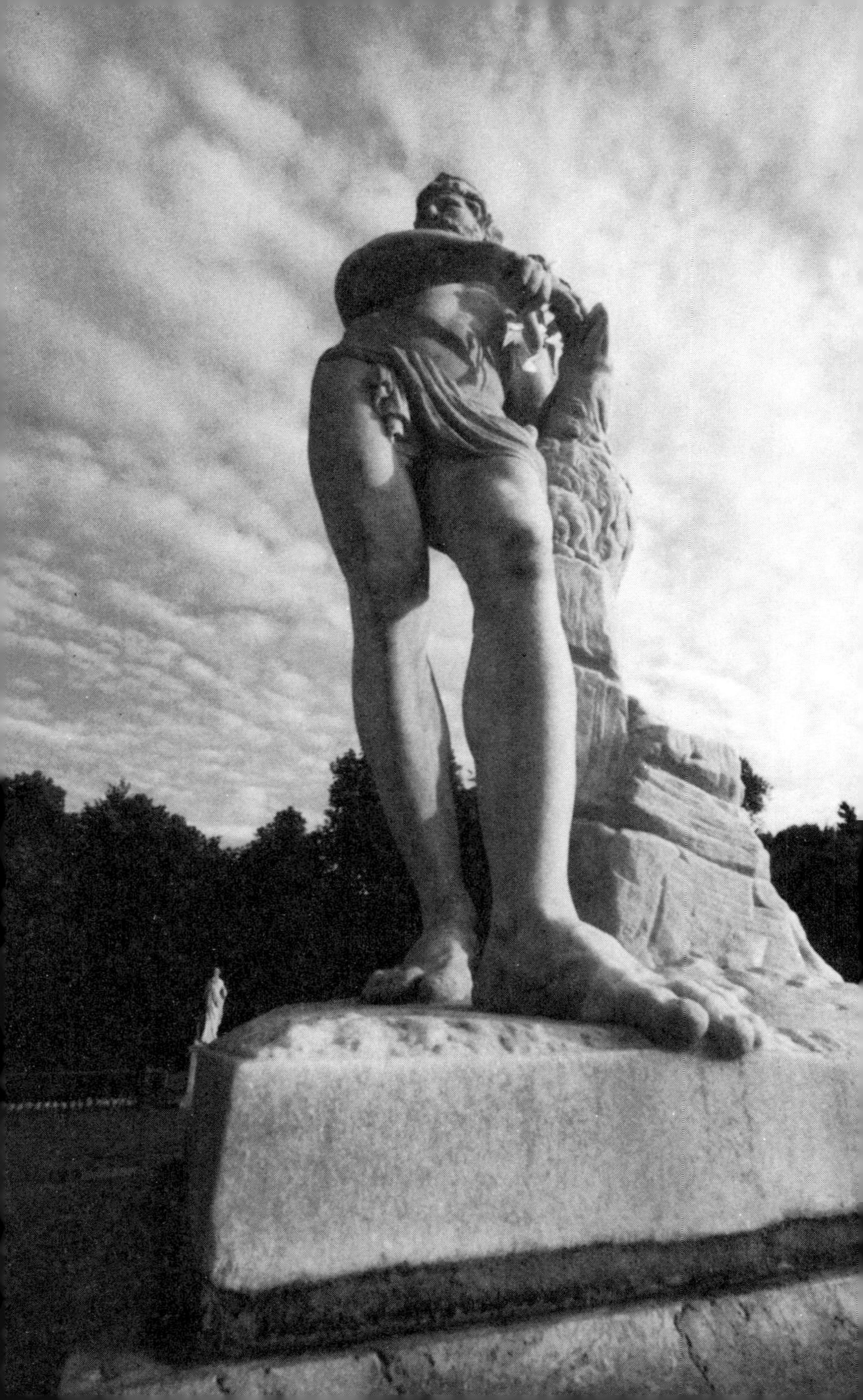

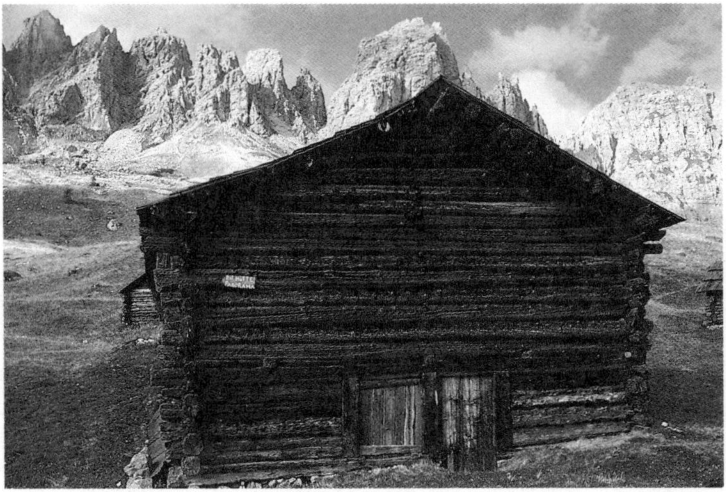

Centre-weighted exposure metering registered the dark wooden wall and selected an exposure which is a little too generous for the background. But because the hut takes up the largest part of the shot, the light background doesn't appear intrusive.

The base of the sculpture is, of course, not nearly as large as the photograph would lead us to believe. A super wide-angle lens used at very close range is responsible for the distortion. The wide depth of field of these lenses made it possible for the sculpture to be shown in focus from top to bottom.

Working Aperture Metering - only if absolutely necessary

Naturally the Nikon FE2, too, is suitable for open aperture metering. But there are some exceptions where this method cannot be applied.

If you wish to attach lenses without AI coupling but with auto iris you can work with or without automatic exposure.

The two paths to correct exposure are as follows; set shutter speed dial to A, select the desired aperture and stop the lens down to the desired value by pressing the depth of field preview lever. Release the shutter. The camera meters the light coming in through the closed aperture and selects a suitable shutter speed.

The second method is to hold in the depth of field preview lever. You can now determine the correct exposure by altering the aperture and/or shutter speed - the two pointers in the viewfinder show the way - then release the depth of field preview lever and take the shot.

If your lens has no auto iris, you will not need the depth of field preview lever. Turning the aperture ring affects the aperture of the lens and the amount of light coming in through the closed-down aperture is received by the exposure meter when the shutter release button is pressed. A suitable speed is selected automatically. But you can also select shutter speed and aperture manually if you follow the guidance of the pointers in the viewfinder. This exposure metering method is required for some bellows (a Novoflex automatic bellows is easier) as well as for the perspective control lenses, also known as shift lenses. For these lenses the exposure must be calculated and stored, using the memory lock, before the lens is shifted to avoid errors.

There are also lenses that have no variable aperture, let alone an automatic iris. These are the mirror lenses which cannot be stopped down. In this case use aperture priority, or work manually. Pressing the shutter release button lightly shows the shutter speed suitable for the fixed lens, pressing the button down fully effects the correct exposure.

You will also have no aperture when using the Nikon FE2 for astral photography with a telescope or in conjunction with a microscope. Here, too, aperture priority is recommended as the shutter speeds are controlled steplessly while with manual control you only have whole steps available.

Compensation with Memory Lock - safe and fast

The memory lock lever lies very conveniently within reach of the right middle finger. When pressed, the preselected shutter speed is stored automatically. But the exposure meter must first be activated by lightly pressing the shutter release button.

The memory lock is very suitable for the correction of individual shots as the main subject or a substitute subject is metered and the corresponding shutter speed is stored. If an entire series needs to be corrected, however, using the exposure compensation facility is more effective.

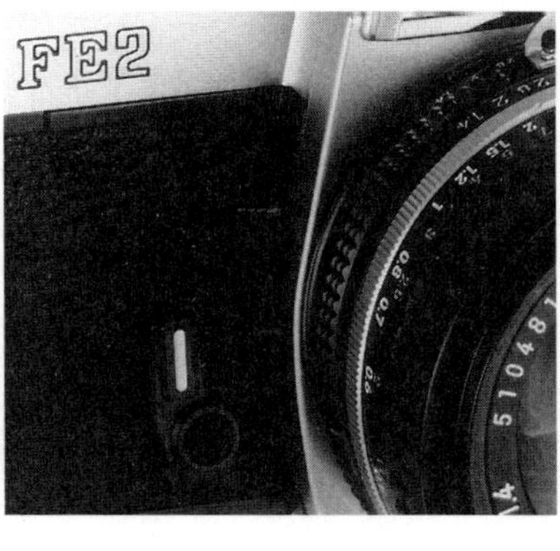

Viewed head-on, the depth of field preview lever is located to the left of the slightly protruding lens mount. Also to the left: the self-timer/memory lock lever.

Exposure Compensation - for entire series

Available compensation factors range from +/- 2 exposure stops in one-third stop increments. Photographing in snow requires a plus compensation in order for the snow not to appear greyish in the picture, and a uniformed chauffeur in front of a black limousine needs a minus compensation for the black to remain black. This applies to colour slides. Negative films, because of their wider exposure range, react to compensation factors differently and any corrections which are visible in the negative are filtered out in the processing laboratory. Select the required compensation factors by first pressing the exposure compensation dial lock (to the left of the viewfinder prism) and then turning the exposure compensation dial. The +/- symbol will appear on the right-hand side of the viewfinder. However, the full range of compensation factors cannot be utilized for all film speeds. For example, at ISO 12/12°, only a plus compensation of 1 stop is possible. At ISO 4000/37°, only a minus compensation of 1 stop.

This in effect increases the film speed range, as a longer exposure by 1 stop for ISO 12/12° is equivalent to the correct exposure for ISO 6/9°. At the other end of the scale a setting of ISO 4000/37° and a minus compensation by 1 stop allows an ISO 8000/37° film to be exposed correctly.

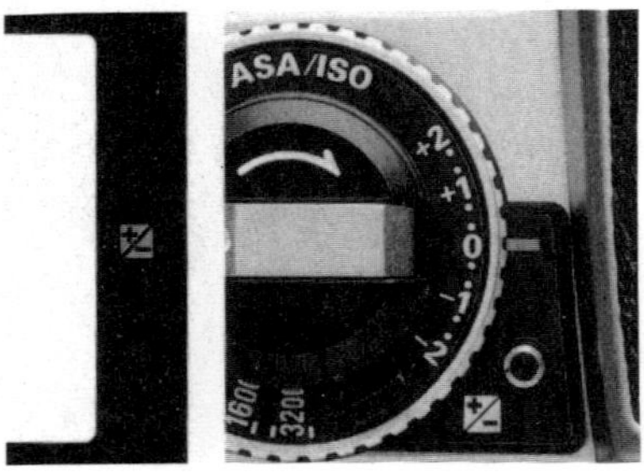

Exposure compensation is possible at pre-determined factors between +2 and -2. The compensation factors are subdivided in one-third steps.

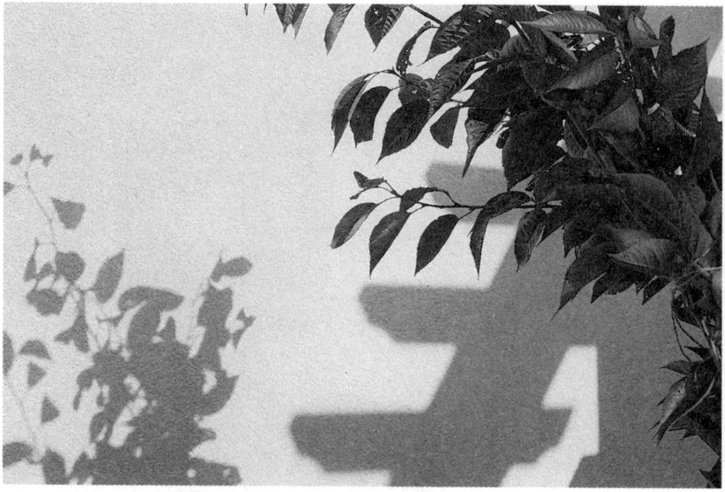

A very light wall becomes grey if you rely on the exposure meter. A plus compensation - easily achieved by metering a section in the shade and storing the metered result - makes the wall appear light in the shot.

To set the film speed, lift up the film speed dial and turn it until the desired speed click-stops opposite the red index dot.

A look at the dial will tell you the speed of the film loaded, but not any information regarding the type. To overcome this problem insert the lid of the film carton into the memo holder on the camera back.

TTL Flash Control - automatically and with fast speeds

Many photographers worry about flash photography. Although using a flash following the guide number method, especially with computer flash, should be no problem. After each flash the question remains over whether a mistake has been made somewhere. TTL exposure metering ends even this worry.

The Nikon FE2 offers TTL flash metering and control if used in conjunction with appropriate flashguns, such as the Speedlight SB-16B. Important for good flash photographs: the main reflector can be tilted, and a small auxiliary reflector can fill in any shadows which might appear.

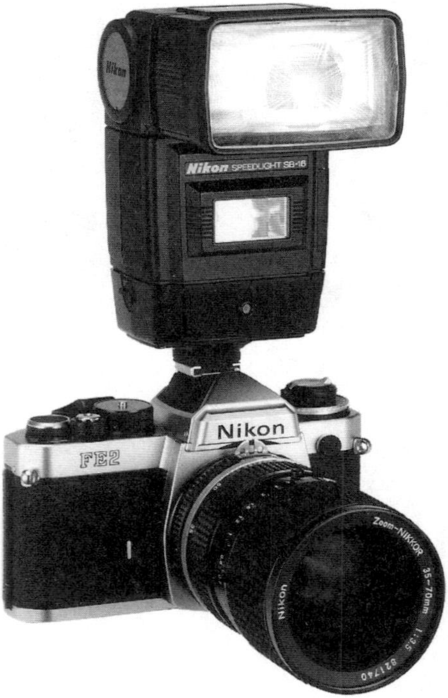

TTL metering of continuous light was old hat when the FE2 came on the market. The Photomic viewfinders for the Nikon F already assessed the light coming from the subject through the lens into the camera. The light from a flash is a different matter. Electronic flash units feature lighting speeds from $^1/_{1000}$ to $^1/_{50000}$ sec. In order to meter and control this light the metering cells must be very sensitive and the electronic controls very fast.

With the appearance of the FE2, Nikon was already using TTL flash control for the professional F3 and the middle range FG.

The advantage of TTL flash control is that in principle any aperture and any film speed can be used for flash photography and that the flash is electronically

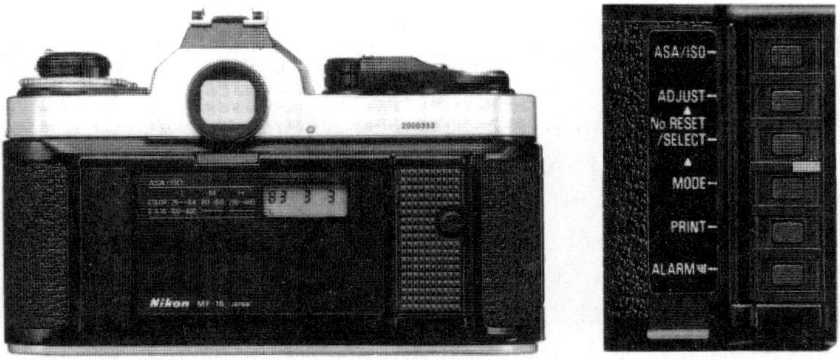

The data back can be fitted or removed in a single movement. Programming is somewhat more elaborate and is carried out by means of buttons. The data is shown on a small LCD panel.

switched off as soon as the film has been exposed sufficiently. This technology has its limits, of course; if the distance to the subject is too short, the duration of the flash can be too long and the subject will be overexposed. On the other hand if the subject is too far away from the camera or the aperture selected is too small, the flash will not be powerful enough to ensure correct exposure. But this problem is not limited to TTL flash control. Flash units controlled manually according to the guide number and computer flash units arrive at the same hurdle.

TTL flash control has a number of other advantages. A flash-ready LED lights up in the viewfinder when the flash is charged. At the same time the shutter speed of $^1/_{250}$ is set automatically - the fastest sync speed available on the Nikon FE2. This means that the FE2 is synchronized faster than any other SLR camera of its time, faster even than the FM2 which only had $^1/_{200}$ sec. For manual selection of the shutter speed, speeds slower than $^1/_{250}$ sec are available for flash photography. Only faster speeds cannot be accepted and are automatically converted to $^1/_{250}$ sec by the camera.

Nothing in the viewfinder after flash exposure indicates correct exposure. If the ready light starts flashing the power of the flash was insufficient and you either need to open the aperture wider or go closer to the subject.

If it flashes before the shot, the film speed setting on the camera and on the flash might not correspond, or you might have switched the flash unit to TTL operation but the camera to the mechanically-controlled $^{1}/_{250}$ sec or "B" setting. Or the camera selector switch on the flash unit is set to B for use with a Nikon EM and not to A for use with other Nikon SLR cameras.

Features - comprehensive and practice-orientated

Those who know the Nikon FM, FE or FM2 will have no difficulty with the Nikon FE2. Despite a few differences, the major elements are the same in all four models.

The film advance lever...
...at the top right of the camera is only used to wind on the film, to cock the shutter and to lock the shutter release. The exposure meter is no longer switched on with this lever.

The multiple exposure lever...
...is situated underneath the film advance lever. When pulled backwards while operating the film advance lever the film will not be wound on and the frame counter not activated. The shutter is cocked, however, allowing another shot on the last exposed frame.

The frame counter...
... lies in front of the film advance lever and counts forwards. When the camera back is opened the counter resets to S and, in automatic mode, the shutter speed is fixed at $^{1}/_{250}$ sec. Once a film is loaded wind it on to 1 for the first shot.

The shutter release button...
...at the right front of the camera top also serves as the switch for the exposure meter. It has a socket for the connection of a cable release, but no outer thread for cable releases with Leica bells. The shutter release button has a third function which is to check the battery. When the shutter button is pressed lightly and then released again very quickly you can observe if the metering index in the viewfinder moves at all. If there is only brief movement or none at all you either need to change the battery or switch to the emergency speed of $^{1}/_{250}$ sec.

The shutter speed dial...
...to the right of the viewfinder prism is large and easy to operate. It locks into the A setting for aperture priority. To rotate the dial if you want to enter a specific shutter speed, the mechanically-controlled emergency speed, or the B setting, first press the locking button in the centre of the dial.

The accessory shoe...
...of the Nikon FE2, apart from the hot contact for cableless activation of flash units, also features three more contact points for automatic conversion to the sync speed, the TTL control and the flash ready LEDs in the viewfinder. Ensure that the contact points are kept clean.

The film speed/exposure compensation dial...
...at the top left is pulled up to set the film speeds. To select a compensation factor just press the exposure compensation dial lock and rotate the dial.

The film rewind knob...
...is located on top of the dial just mentioned. Pull out and turn the film rewind crank to rewind the exposed film back into its cassette, even if motor drive MD-12 is

attached to the camera. This only advances the film, it does not rewind it. When the rewind knob is pulled up the back cover opens if...

The camera back lock lever...
...under the rewind knob is pushed sideways.

The sync terminal...
...for connecting sync cables is located at the right front of the camera.

The lens release button...
...is on the right of the lens mount while at the same level on the other side is ...

The depth of field preview lever...
...which is important in connection with the composition of the picture and metering at working aperture.

The self-timer/memory lock lever...
...on the left front (seen from the front) has two functions. Pushing it away from the lens activates the self-timer. The sequence starts when the shutter release button is pressed. Exposure occurs after about 10 sec. The mirror swings up when the shutter release button is pressed which allows the self-timer to be used as a guard against camera shake. If you change your mind before releasing the shutter simply return the self-timer lever to its original position. But if the sequence has already started, this action will cause the shutter to be released. When this lever is pushed towards the lens the exposure value can be stored, which is useful for high contract subjects.

The battery chamber...
...in the base of the camera holds two button cells (1.5V alkaline-manganese or 1.55V silver-oxide) or one 3V lithium battery which has the advantage of with-

standing longer rest or storage periods and functioning better in cold weather. In very low temperatures use the Anti-cold Battery Pack DB-2.

The tripod socket...
...is located on the optical axis giving the camera and lens good stability. It has a $\frac{1}{4}$" thread. The socket also accepts the motor drive which has a tripod socket of its own.

The film rewind button...
...in the camera base has to be pressed to release the take-up spool mechanism.

The motor drive contacts...
...on the left and right of the camera base allow the direct coupling of motor drive MD-12 to the Nikon FE2.

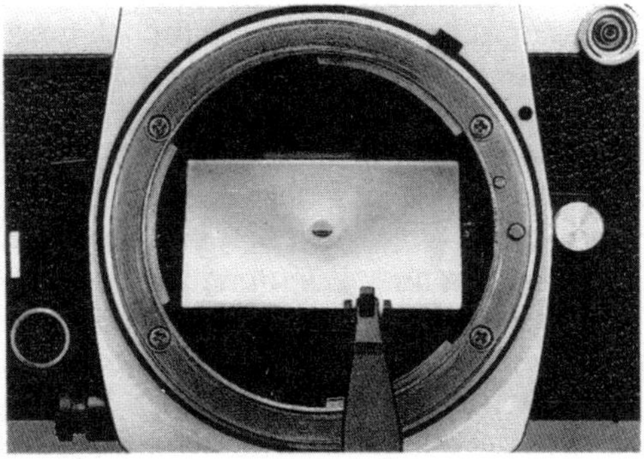

The focusing screen can be exchanged by the photographer. Three variations are available.

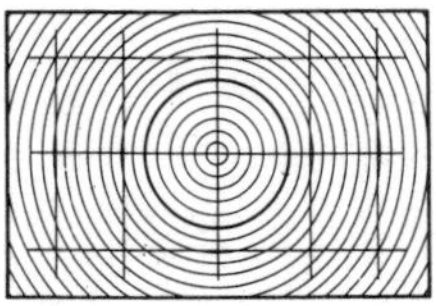

E2

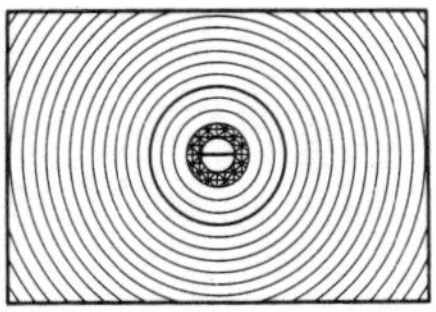

K2

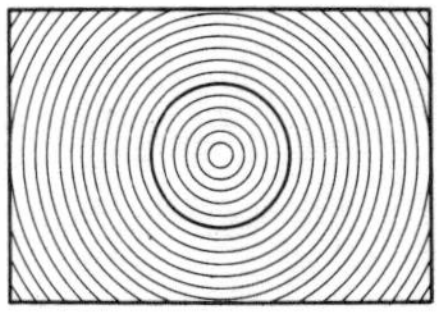

B2

The focusing screen...

...can be seen when the lens is removed. It covers the mirror compartment. The standard screen K2 consists of a split-image rangefinder with microprism ring. There are two replacement screens available - interchangeable by using the tweezers provided - the B2 matt/Fresnel focusing screen for use with slow lenses, telescopes and microscopes and the E2 matt/Fresnel screen with vertical and horizontal lines for accurate aligning of the camera for copying or architectural shots. This screen is also excellent for use with PC Nikkor lenses.

Nikon FA - Leader in Multi-Pattern Metering

The year 1983 was an interesting year for Nikon users. The Nikon FE2 with its sync speed of $^1/_{250}$ sec was introduced. Two years ahead of the Minolta 7000, the Nikon F3 AF and two special lenses allowed true autofocus photography in the SLR field. The Nikon L35AF, a compact camera, came on the market. And the year also saw the birth of the Nikon FA with its multi-pattern metering system - a system regarded as rather exotic at the time but indispensable in the top range SLR cameras of today.

The Nikon FA is a very comprehensively-equipped camera. It features TTL flash control as well as motor drive and data back facility. As you would expect from Nikon the FA is also integrated in the existing system. Emphasis is laid on the lens connection. Almost all the lenses and converters built by Nikon for use with SLR cameras can be attached to the Nikon FA, but there are a few exceptions.

Only when F Nikkor lenses with AI-S connection (including the modern AF lenses) or E series lenses are used can all the possibilities offered by this camera be fully utilized.

AI-S lenses are recognizable by the orange coloured highest f/number (smallest aperture), and a focal length indexing ridge in the bayonet which informs the camera whether the focal length of the lens is shorter than 105mm or longer than 135mm, a lens type signal notch, and lens speed indexing post - important aspects in connection with the automatic functions of the camera. AI-S lenses can be used in conjunction with older Nikon SLR cameras as they also feature the

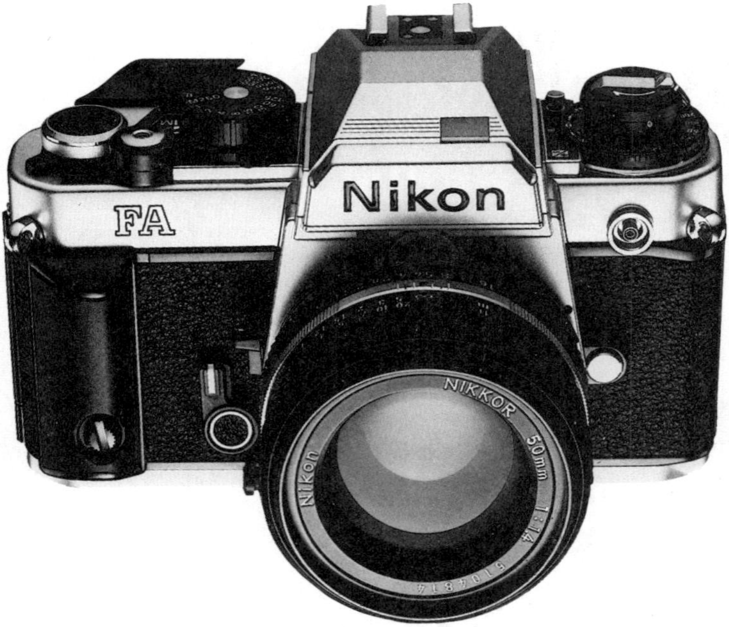

The Nikon FA marked a high point in the production of cameras with manually-focused lenses. It incorporated almost everything needed for good photography.

typical meter coupling prong. E series lenses do not have meter coupling prongs and so can only be used with AI cameras (Nikkormat FT3, Nikon EL2, F2-A Photomic, F2-AS Photomic and FM).

Automatic Multi-Pattern Petering (AMP) - with or without

The exposure meter of the Nikon FA divides the scene into five segments, then reads each segments's brightness separately. The evaluation of the different metered values is the feature that sets the Nikon FA apart.

The camera's microcomputer stores many possible meter results and also the information on what to do

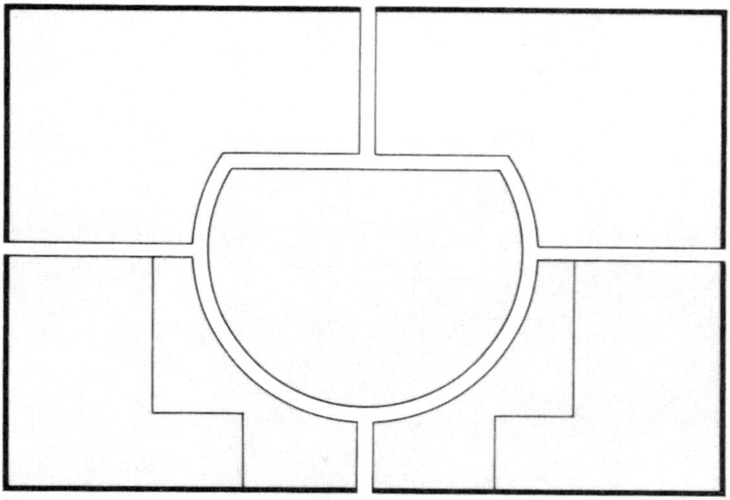

Multi-pattern metering was a development which was met with a great deal of misunderstanding when the Nikon FA was introduced. The exposure is metered in five segments, and the camera can recognise any necessary corrections by comparing the individual results. The central metering area can also be used on its own - the exposure is then metered with Nikon's traditional centre weighting: 60% at the centre and 40% towards the edges.

when the same result appears again. For example, you are taking a picture of your partner on the beach, before a bright sky with some passing clouds. The central metering area calculates a low light value (where your partner stands in his own shadow), the four outer metering areas calculate high values (where the bright sky determines the exposure). AMP metering recognizes the back-lit situation and compensates the exposure total towards plus, i.e. the main subject is lightened and is defined in the picture, the surrounding areas are also reproduced lighter but still acceptably as the AMP metering does not base the calculation solely on the main subject. In normal metering the bright surroundings would have dazzled the exposure meter. The sky would appear nice and light but the main subject would be much too dark.

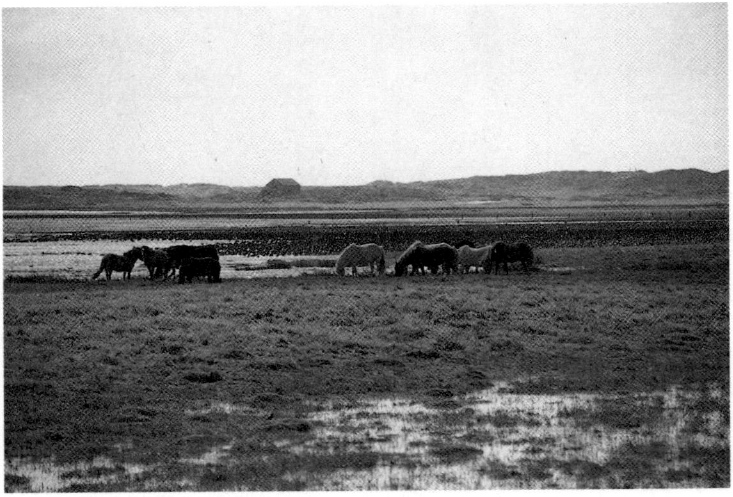

A backlit subject which needs no further compensation, thanks to multi-pattern metering. Naturally, even the automatic mode cannot prevent the sky being reproduced very light.

AMP metering is geared to solve many such difficult situations and provides an exposure which takes into account all the prevalent contrasts and the general brightness of the picture. Occasionally AMP metering works too well, though, and does not realize that you intend to reproduce the main subject as a silhouette or that you wish the dark clouds to add drama to the photograph. In this case simply select the centre weighted integrating metering, by pressing the change-over switch on the front left below the lens mount (seen from the front) and set shutter speed and aperture manually. For several shots with centre weighted metering lock the button by turning it forwards.

With the AMP and centre weighted metering options there should be no subject that cannot be tackled with the Nikon FA.

The exposure meter is activated by lightly pressing the shutter release button.

Exposure Compensation - manually

When the camera realizes that the subject deviates from the average value of 18% reflectivity it follows a preset pattern and compensates the exposure to achieve an optimally exposed picture.

There is no need to rely on these corrections created by the camera automatically - you can enter your own compensation factors. The exposure can be compensated by +/-2 stops which can be set on the compensation scale to the right of the viewfinder prism. To avoid inadvertent compensation the dial is locked and to release it press the dial lock. The compensation factors can also be used to expose correctly a film outside the speed range of ISO 12/12° to ISO 4000/37°. The range can be increased from ISO 6/9° to ISO 8000/40°.

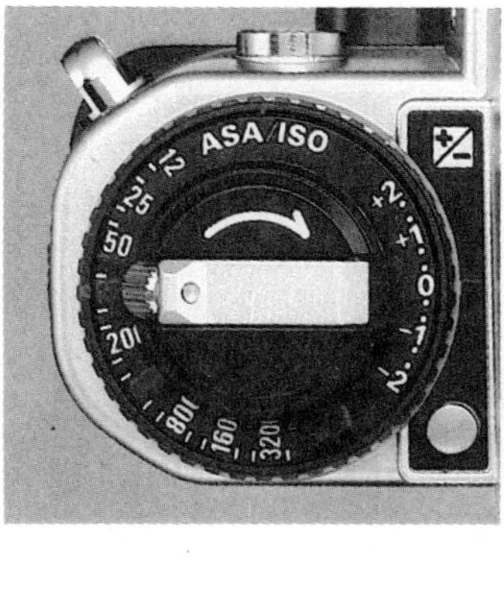

The dial at the top left-hand side of the camera is used for film speed selection (DX-coding did not become established until later). It is also used to carry out exposure compensation in one-third steps between +2 and -2.

You should only use the compensation factors in connection with centre weighted metering and, of course, only with one of the automatic exposure functions. To avoid compensating more than necessary the +/- symbol lights up in the viewfinder to remind you of the compensation factor set.

Program Automatic - two variations but no choice

Program automatic is probably the most debated form of automatic exposure, especially in a camera directed mainly at the experienced photographer.

The program automatic controls aperture and shutter speed - and takes away, as the critics say, any form of creativity on behalf of the photographer. This is rubbish, of course. Although the photographer cannot select a specific shutter speed to freeze or blur movement and he cannot specify the extent of the depth of field by preselecting a suitable aperture he has the opportunity to select the best framing, perhaps by circling the subject or by chosing a special lens, while the camera takes care of shutter speed and aperture. This participation from the photographer is extremely important as the camera itself is not creative. Apart from that the Nikon FA allows you to select shutter speed and aperture in other ways and many subjects require neither a specific aperture nor a certain shutter speed in order to make an effective picture anyway.

Program automatic does not mean that the camera selects shutter speed and aperture at random but it is what its name says - a very precise, preset program (two programs in the case of the Nikon FA). AI-S and E series lenses inform the camera if the focal length is shorter than 105mm or longer than 135mm and a normal or a fast program is selected accordingly. The normal program starts, for example, with the shutter speed/aperture combination of 1 sec and f/1.4 when a 50mm,f/1.4 lens, an ISO 100/21° film and very low light (EV1) are used. The aperture remains fully open up to EV4 and only the shutter speed is increased and from EV5 onwards shutter speed and aperture are controlled simultaneously - in half stop increments. The cut-off point therefore lies at $^{1}/_{8}$ sec and f/1.4 which is not really practice-orientated. It would be better to keep the

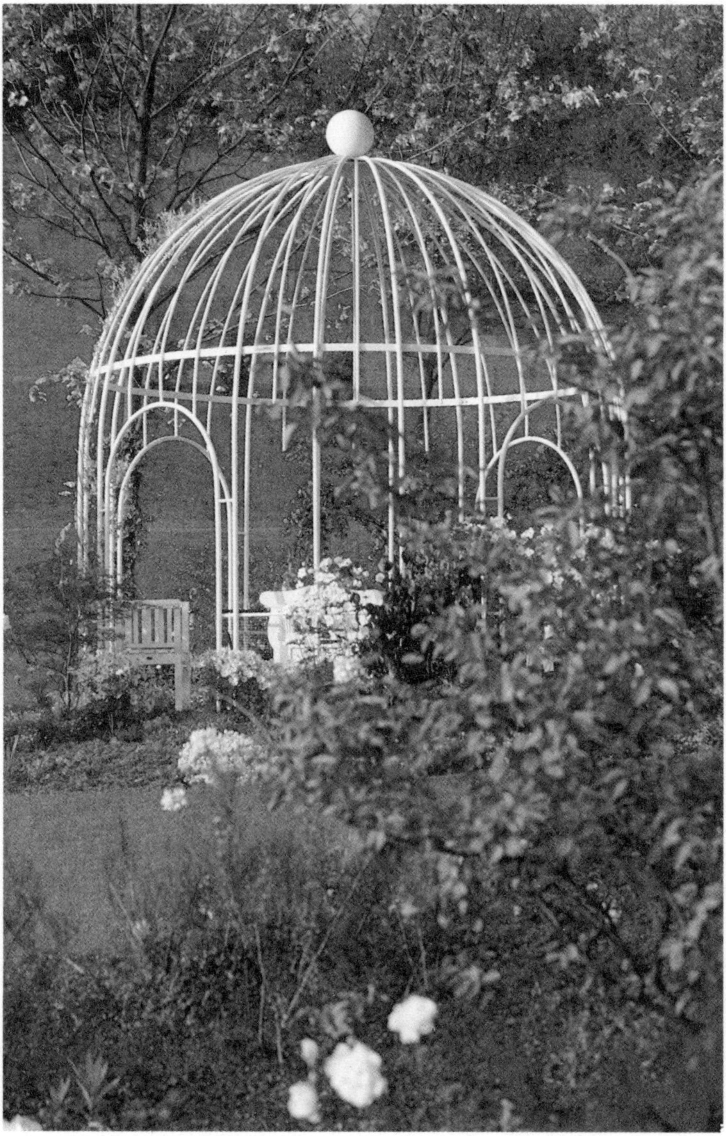

The automatic program for exposure control is perfectly suited to subjects such as this.

aperture open until $^1/_{60}$ sec and a low EV can be achieved as it is then possible to use a 50mm lens hand-held without the danger of camera shake. The cut-off point also applies to other f/1.4 lenses such as the 85mm,f/1.4 portrait telephoto. When using this lens the program automatic will select $^1/_8$ sec and f/1.4 for a correctly-exposed picture - but it will be blurred by camera shake.

The fast program is arranged in such a way that the combination of $^1/_{4000}$ sec and f/11 is given when a 200mm,f/4 lens, an ISO 100 film and a high exposure value (EV20) are used. From this point shutter speed and aperture are controlled together until a combination of $^1/_{500}$ sec and f/4 is reached at EV13. But this lens requires the exposure to be controlled via the speed as there is no greater focal length available. In the case of a 135mm,f/2 telephoto, shutter speed and aperture are changed up to $^1/_{125}$ sec and f/2. This makes sense as at $^1/_{500}$ sec a 200mm lens, and at $^1/_{125}$ sec a 135mm lens, can still be hand-held without camera shake. If you are using a 200mm,f/2.8 telephoto with the Nikon FA it becomes more difficult as $^1/_{125}$ sec with 200mm focal length signifies camera shake blur.

But this should not be reason enough to reject program automatic out of hand - just use it wisely. Wide-angle and telephoto lenses of normal focal length can be used without any problems. The giants and lenses of medium focal length (from 50mm to 135mm) must be used cautiously when in the program mode. It is always wise to check the automatically-selected shutter speed in the viewfinder LCD panel.

You can get more 'live action' holiday shots by venturing down a side street, away from the tourist masses streaming towards the famous sights, than by devoting your efforts exclusively to postcard views.

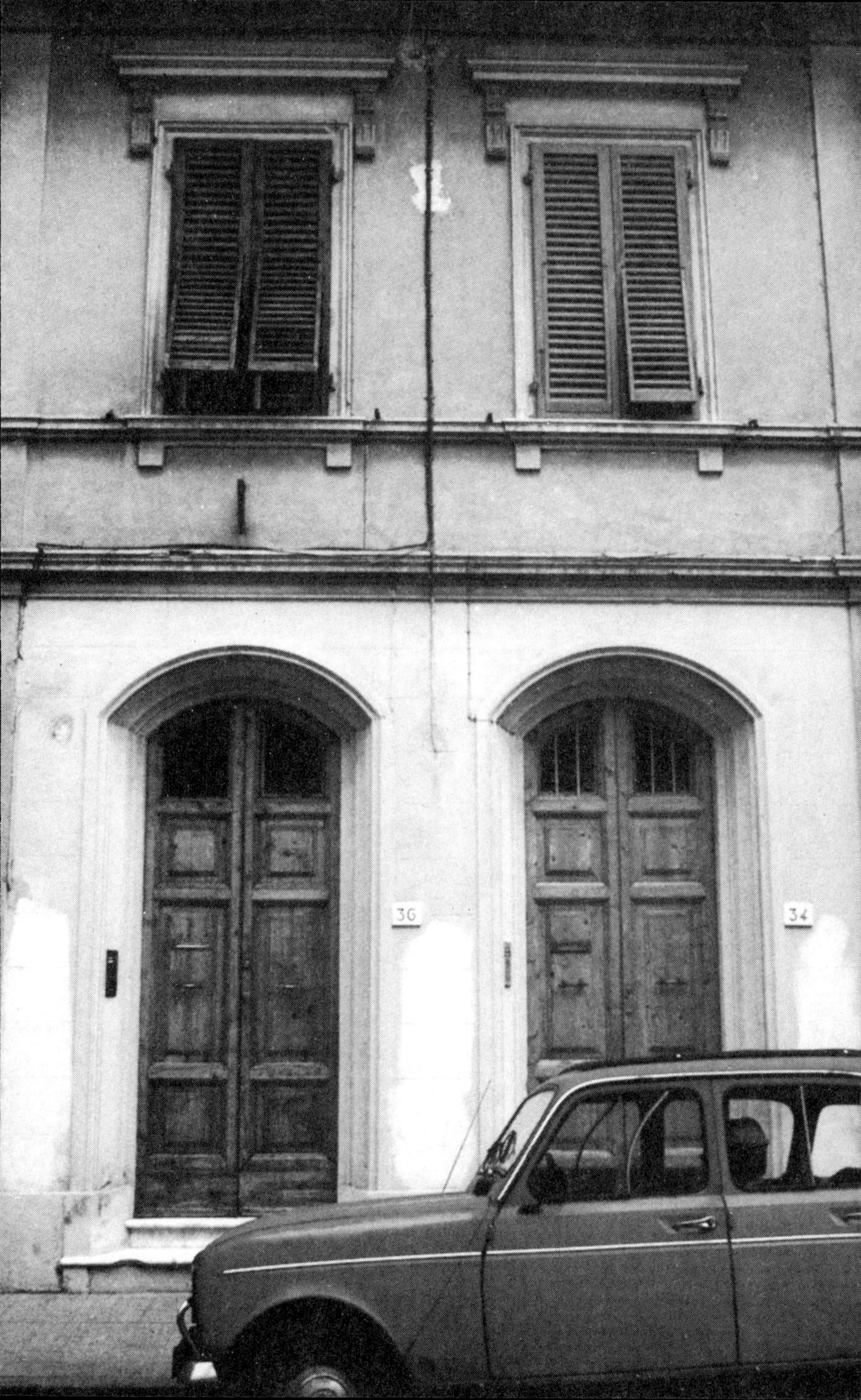
36
34

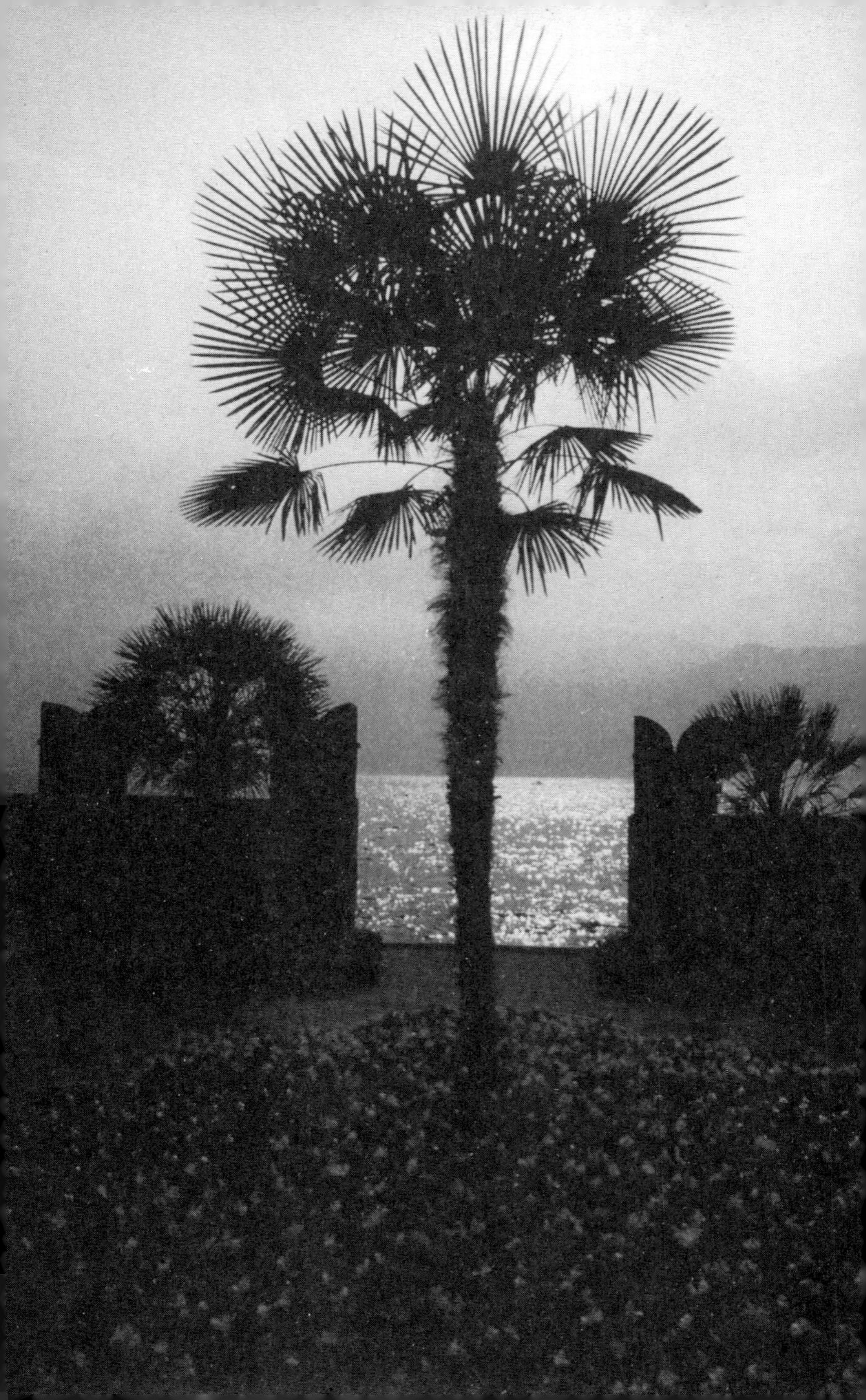

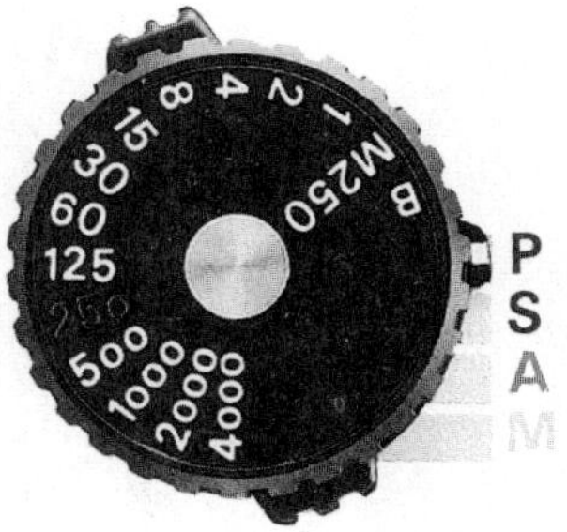

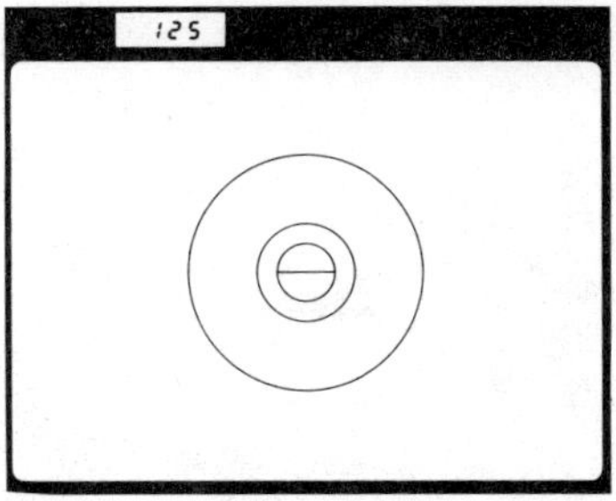

Simply select 'P' for automatic program on the shooting mode index, although two programs are available. The camera decides whether to use the standard or high-speed program depending on the focal lenght of the lens - this information is mechanically transmitted from the lens into the damera body. The shutter speed is indicated in the viewfinder, but not the aperture.

In order to use program automatic you must first set the shooting mode index, a small lever underneath the shutter speed dial, to P and the aperture ring to the smallest aperture. If you omit to do the latter the viewfinder LCD will show FEE instead of the shutter speed. This does not necessarily lead to wrongly exposed pictures, but there is only a reduced aperture range available to the camera - from full aperture to the value the aperture ring is set to.

For a long time photographers had to stick to the rule 'sun behind you, press the shutter' if they wanted correctly exposed shots without flare. Nowadays improved lenses can produce good shots even if the sun do appear in it and, thanks to a narrow metering angle and metering result storage, adjusting the exposure isn't a problem.

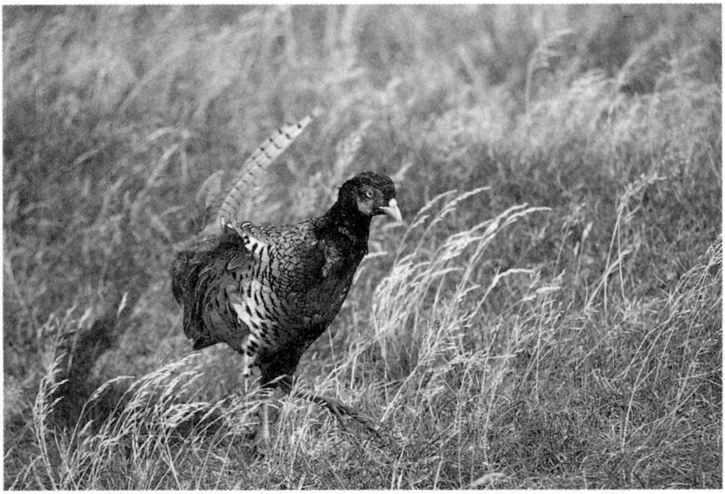

If a lens with a longer focal length than 135mm is used, the high-speed program is automatically activated. The narrow depth of field of the wide aperture separates the subject from the background, the fast shutter speed prevents camera shake.

Aperture Priority - already known

To use aperture priority set the mode index to A. Select the aperture on the aperture ring of the lens and the Nikon FA automatically sets the shutter speed according to the brightness and film speed - no matter which way you turn the shutter speed dial. The only point is that it must not be set to the mechanical emergency speed of $^1/_{250}$ sec or to B.

Aperture priority allows you to decide on the depth of field - either shallow for portraits, flowers, landscape details or wider for panorama views, objects, and snapshots. To judge the effect of the picture, press the depth of field preview lever.

Like the Nikon FM2 and FE2 the Nikon FA also features $^1/_{4000}$ sec as the fastest shutter speed. This allows you to open the aperture fully even if the brightness is very high and/or you are using a high speed film. The danger of overexposure at speeds of $^1/_{2000}$ or $^1/_{4000}$ sec is rare.

The viewfinder LCD shows the automatically-selected shutter speed mode, while beside it the ADR window shows the preset f/number. If the $^1/_{4000}$ sec is not enough to control the brightness, the LCD panel will show HI. In this case you will have to close the aperture or to use a slower film or a neutral density filter. The display will show Lo when a shutter speed of 1 sec is not sufficient to bring enough light to the film. Remedies are a larger aperture, a faster film, or artificial light from light bulbs or flash.

Also select the A setting when you need to meter the exposure with working aperture because no matter whether the lens has an auto iris or a preset aperture - aperture priority will work. Simply press the depth of field preview lever and the shutter release. Manual centre weighted metering, too, is possible with working aperture whereas only automatic aperture lenses can be used in the P and S settings.

Shutter Speed Priority - enough time for speed

Set the mode index to S for shutter speed priority and the aperture ring to the smallest aperture. Select a shutter speed on the shutter speed dial and the Nikon FA selects a suitable aperture indicating this in the viewfinder LCD. To avoid misunderstandings, the aperture is shown together with the letter "f" for f/number. The shutter speed is visible at the top right of the viewfinder image.

It can happen, however, that correct exposure cannot be achieved with the preselected shutter speed - when it is too bright for even the smallest aperture or too dark for even the largest aperture. In both cases the camera automatically switches to cybernetic override and

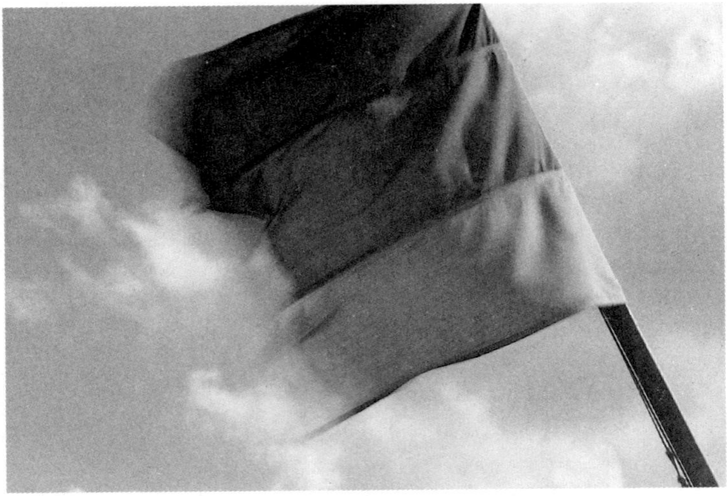

By selecting a suitable shutter speed the fluttering of the flag can be shown clearly in the shot.

controls the shutter speed by speeding it up in the first case and slowing it down in the second. You can observe what is happening as instead of the aperture the viewfinder LCD will indicate the shutter speed. This override function cannot be valued enough. It allows you to set a shutter speed you think right and if this speed is not possible the camera remains as close to your value as possible.

If even after using the override function correct exposure is impossible to achieve you are warned of overexposure by the letters HI and of underexposure by the letters Lo. To avoid this use a slower or faster film, a neutral density filter or artificial light. To remind you that you have not set the lens to its smallest aperture the LCD indicates FEE.

There are 13 values from 1 to $^{1}/_{4000}$ sec available for shutter speed priority. Intermediate values are not possible.

The choice of shutter speed depends on the subject

but can also be determined by the lens. The so-called hand-held formula will tell you - slowest speed for sharp hand-held pictures = 1 divided by focal length in mm.

As you may know you could avoid camera shake and still use a slower speed even without tripod. Hold the camera against a wall, column or a lamp post, or place it on a balustrade, a garden fence or a seat back. You have a little more freedom with a long lens when you support the lens with your camera bag and place both on a firm surface.

Manual Exposure Control - centre weighted or not

If you prefer to select shutter speed and aperture yourself set the mode index to M, choose speed and aperture and watch the LCD in the viewfinder. The shutter speed will be shown as well as the +/- symbols which warn of over or underexposure. Adjust shutter speed and/or aperture until both symbols light up together. The aperture appears in the ADR window.

This allows you to achieve correct exposure - based on centre weighted integrating metering to which the camera switches automatically when in M mode.

But it is nonsense to achieve correct exposure by manually selecting shutter speed and aperture - the program automatic can do this much quicker. Manual exposure control is recommended when you deliberately want to deviate from the correct exposure values to create certain effects.

A special method of manual exposure control is to use the mechanically-selected emergency speed of $^{1}/_{250}$ sec or the B setting.

Normally the Nikon FA's shutter is controlled electromagnetically and when the batteries have run out it and the exposure meter stop functioning. But by pressing the M250/B lock button on the camera back and setting the speed dial to M250 you can use the $^{1}/_{250}$ sec and, if you are lucky, one of the apertures on the lens will match. Ordinary colour negative films with a wide exposure range will give you extra safety. Slide films or high-performance colour negative films require very accurate exposure, however, and should be used in the powerless camera only in conjunction with a hand-held exposure meter.

The B setting also can only be selected when the lock button is pressed. In the B setting the shutter remains open until the shutter release button is released. To avoid camera shake use a cable release. The exposure for slow pictures can be calculated with a hand-held exposure meter but this is not required for many situations. If, for example, you want to photograph a firework display, choose f/11 for an ISO 100 film, f/16 for an ISO 200 film, aim the camera, and wait until the rockets explode. And to be on the safe side take a few shots with different shutter speeds or in the B setting with different apertures.

Flash - TTL with fast speeds

The Nikon FA is also equipped with an additional metering sensor in the bottom of the mirror chamber which receives the light reflected from the surface of the film. Its purpose is TTL flash control. The advantages of TTL control when using a flash: all apertures are available enabling you to adjust the depth of field to the subject; flash exposure without complicated calculation; setting, resetting and transfer of values is as accurate as normal exposure; even fill-in flashing creates no problems.

TTL flash units by Nikon such as the SB-15, SB-16B and SB-18 are ideal to bring light into the darkness. The fastest sync speed for electronic flash units on the

Nikon FA is $^1/_{250}$ sec. This is automatically selected when the flash is ready. In order to get a slower speed for flash operation set the mode index to M. Faster speeds are not possible as the FA automatically converts these to $^1/_{250}$ sec.

As soon as the flash is charged the flash-ready light on the unit and in the camera viewfinder will illuminate. Now set the desired aperture on the lens. Provided the aperture selected is not too small and the subject is not too far away the picture will be lit correctly by the flash. If correct illumination was impossible the ready light in the viewfinder starts to flicker advising you to open the aperture wider or to go closer to the subject.

This procedure will create quite normal flash photographs.

If you want to deviate from the norm you can use the sync speed of $^1/_{250}$ sec for fill-in flash.

Fill-in flash is required when the main subject lies in the shade on a sunny day or it is positioned in front of a very light background which the AMP metering cannot cope with. In most cases setting the mode index to M and adjusting the exposure in such a way that the result is a shutter speed of $^1/_{60}$ sec with a suitable aperture will suffice. If you use the flash with that aperture the main subject will be lit by the flash and the surroundings or background by the normal light reaching the film through the aperture at a speed of $^1/_{60}$ sec.

A sync speed of $^1/_{250}$ sec is also very useful when there is movement in the subject which would not be sharp at $^1/_{60}$ sec. The fast $^1/_{250}$ sec can freeze that movement. In addition the aperture can be opened wider with a short sync speed without the surroundings or background becoming overexposed by the ambient light. That means you can also use a fill-in flash when you want to define the subject by a small depth of field.

Features - all there but still clear

The body of the Nikon FA looks a little different from the shape we known since 1977. The large square viewfinder prism gives a rather striking appearance to the FA which does perhaps not quite match the small handgrip. Numerous operating elements are in the familiar places which is convenient when using two Nikon cameras.

The shutter release button...
...which also serves as the main switch for the exposure meter is at the top right, near the front edge, and can be reached easily with the index finger. The difference between lightly pressing for exposure metering and pressing down fully for actual exposure is clearly noticeable. Only when using the emergency speed of $^1/_{250}$ sec does the shutter release button seem slightly heavy.

The frame counter...
...to the right of the shutter release button counts forwards and is reset automatically when the back cover is opened.

The multiple exposure lever...
...is located underneath the film advance lever and must be pulled backwards after exposure while the film wind lever is operated or the motor drive winds on the film. If you intend to superimpose two full-frame pictures you should compensate the exposure by -1 stop before shooting so that the two pictures together have a normal exposure. If you want to combine two subjects before a black background or plan a *doppelganger* picture each shot must be correctly exposed separately. In the case of the *doppelganger,* metering needs to be conducted before a *doppelganger* mask is attached to the lens. Multiple exposures are also possible. But if

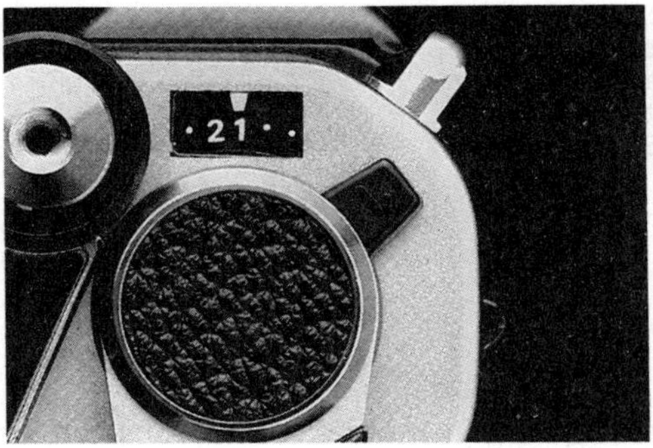

For multiple exposures a lever has to be pulled backwards. The shutter cocking mechanism and film transport are then no longer coupled.

each individual subject is exposed to fill the frame the total picture might turn out to be rather confusing.

The film advance lever...
...at the top right is sharply angled and must be pulled right through to its stop point for the film to be advanced properly.

The shutter speed dial...
...is large and easy to operate although it is quite close to the viewfinder prism. In aperture priority mode it clicks into whole stops and can be moved to the B or $^1/_{250}$ setting only when the M250/B lock button on the camera back is pressed.

The mode selector...
...is a small lever underneath the shutter speed dial, complete with mode index, which can be set to the P, S and A positions for the different modes of automatic exposure and to M for manual exposure control.

The accessory shoe...
...on top of the viewfinder prism features the usual hot shoe contact allowing any flash unit with hot shoe connection to be used - not recommended by Nikon who claim that the high trigger voltage of a non-system

The shooting mode index is located to the right of the shutter speed dial. The camera is here set to aperture priority. The other modes are automatic program ('P'), shutter priority ('S') and manual mode ('M').

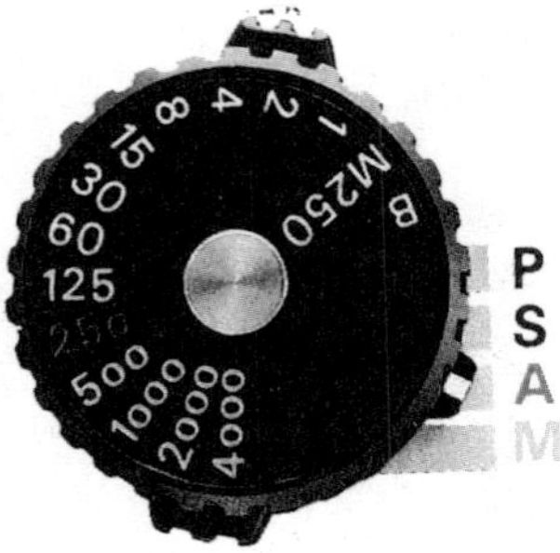

flash unit could damage the camera's electronics. Three further contact points facilitate connection with suitably equipped flash units.

The film speed/exposure compensation dial...
..is on the far left of the camera. By lifting and simultaneous turning of the dial film speeds from ISO 12/12° to ISO 4000/37° can be set in one-third step increments. This dial serves also as the exposure compensation scale where compensation factors within the range of +/-2 stops can be set. Towards each end of the film speed range this decreases. At ISO 12/12° there are only three steps from +1 to -2 available, at ISO 4000/37° from -1 to +2. To select a compensation factor unlock the dial by pressing the dial lock on the right behind it. The +/- symbol in the viewfinder indicates that you are using the exposure compensation facility.

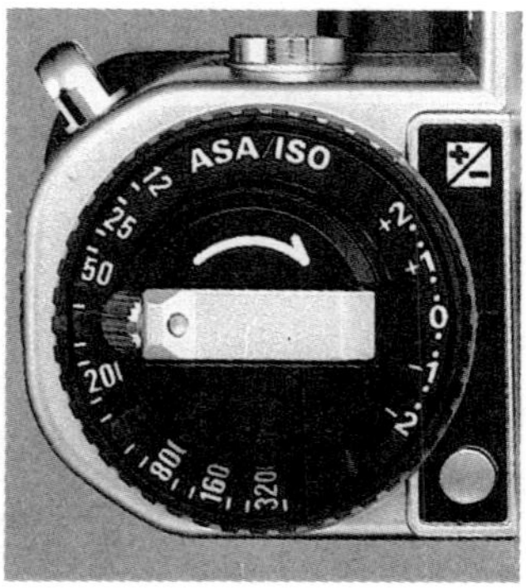

The button on the left has to be pressed first to unlock the dial before an exposure compensation can be selected. The back cover locking lever can be found on the rewind knob. This is designed to avoid inadvertant opening of the back cover.

The film rewind knob and back cover release...
...is located on top of the film speed dial. Before double exposures it is wise to turn the rewind crank a little clockwise in order to make sure the film is taut. Otherwise the crank is used to rewind the film back into its cassette (even when a motor drive is attached). Pulling up the rewind knob after pressing the film rewind button on the base of the camera opens the back cover.

The sync terminal...
...on the front right of the camera (seen from the front) accepts sync cables which should be used when working with studio flash units.

The lens release button...
...is in its usual place on the right side of the lens mount.

The depth of field preview lever...
...is on the front left and is used to check the extent of the depth of field in the viewfinder or when shooting with working aperture metering.

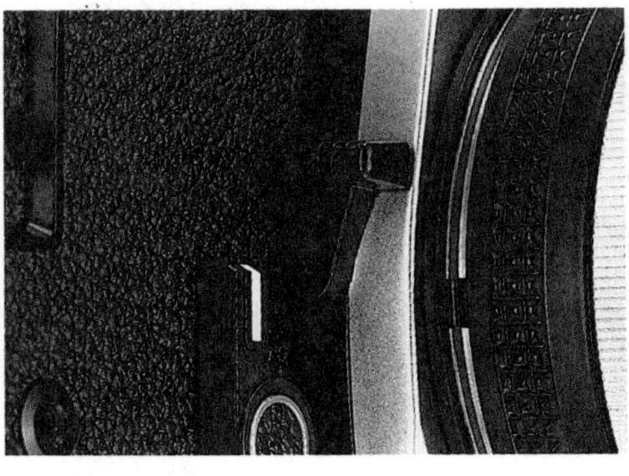

The depth of field preview button is important if the aperture is supposed to determine a depth of field to suit the subject.

The self-timer lever...
...has no dual function on the Nikon FA as this camera does not feature a memory lock function. Push lever away from the lens to cock the self-timer and press the shutter release button to activate it.

The centre weighted metering changeover switch...
...at the bottom left (seen from the front) of the lens mount is important if you want to work with automatic exposure and centre weighted metering. This switch can be locked.

The focusing screen...
...can be seen when the lens is removed and you look slightly upwards into the mirror chamber. The standard screen has a split-image rangefinder and microprism ring which both darken when a lens of f/5.6 or slower is used and also when a more powerful lens is stopped down to check the depth of field. The focusing screen is interchangeable by the user.

The tripod socket...
...in the camera base is also used to couple the motor drive to the camera. The motor drive also has its own tripod socket so you can use both which is quite a good idea. .

The battery chamber...
...with battery clamp accepts two 1.5V alkaline-manganese batteries, two 1.55V silver oxide cells or one 3V lithium battery. The latter is preferable despite its higher price as it allows the camera to be stored for some time or to be used at low temperatures.

The film rewind button...
...on the left of the camera base can also be operated via the motor drive to wind the film back into the cassette.

The two motor drive couplers...
...on the left and right of the camera base connect the motor drive MD-15 to the camera - both mechanically and electronically.

The camera back...
...contains a memo holder and can be replaced by a data back - the MF-12 with cable connection or the MF-16 without cable connection.

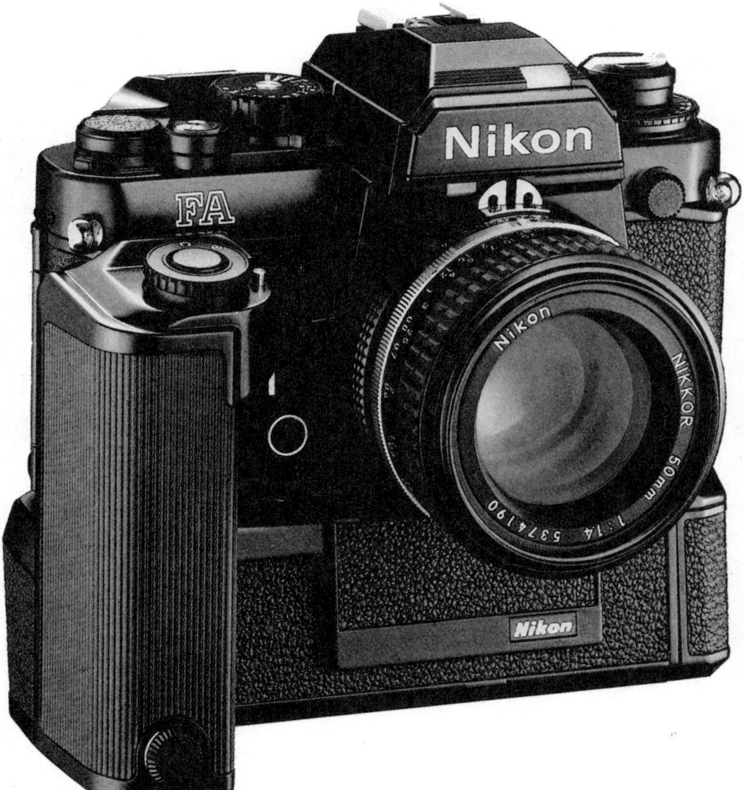

A new motor drive was introduced at the same time as the Nikon FA: the MD-15. With its handgrip the camera handles well. At the bottom of the grip is the connection for remote controls, which only make sense in conjunction with a motor.

The viewfinder eyepiece...

...of the Nikon FA can be closed - important when using a tripod, as light coming in through the eyepiece could alter the exposure metering. Turn the shutter lever to the left of the eyepiece upwards. The shutter is coloured red to remind you that the eyepiece is closed.

The viewfinder eyepiece can be used to attach various accessories such as the right-angle viewing attachment DR-3 for use near the ground or with a copying stand. The eyepiece magnifier DG-2 simplifies focusing especially in macro photography. Eyepiece correction lenses allow you to focus without your spectacles.

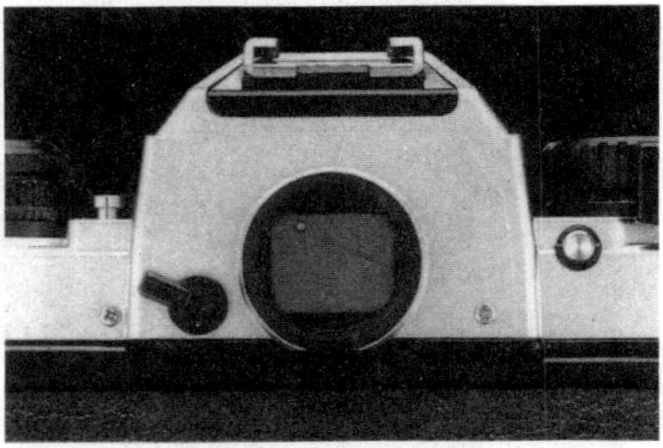

The eyepiece can be covered - an option which is particularly important for tripod shots, preventing light from entering through the eyepiece into the viewfinder, thereby falsifying the exposure metering result.

Lenses - Evolution Not Revolution

The camera body is basically just a dark container into which light can enter for a specific time in order to expose the film inside it. That the film records a picture has nothing to do with the container - this is the task of the lens. Nikon lenses have been renowned for several decades and are always found at the top when tested. The extensive range of more than 70 different lenses can cause some confusion. But when separated into groups the decision for one or the other is not so difficult.

Whereas other manufacturers took the opportunity to introduce new lens series with new types of bayonet when converting from manual focus to autofocus, Nikon remained with the bayonet which has been around in principle since 1959 and the Nikon F and which can be adapted to the requirements of new technology by detail modifications. Sometimes the interior of the lens changed - aperture control, for example, when open aperture metering arrived - but Nikkor lenses can be used with all Nikon SLR cameras.

The Lenses - more and more opportunities

At the beginning there were lenses without auto iris or meter coupling prong. This prong directly affects the diaphragm in the lens. When the aperture control ring is turned the iris diaphragm opens or closes. TTL metering is only possible with working aperture and should be carried out after focusing so that the open aperture provides a bright viewfinder image for focusing.

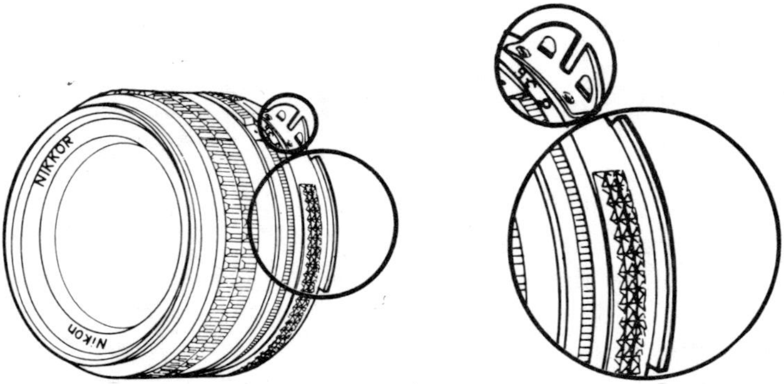

On an AI lens bayonet a coupling ridge takes on the task of informing the exposure meter about the speed of the lens. The meter coupling prong is only used if the AI lens is attached to an older camera without AI connection.

Lenses with auto iris but without meter coupling prong were the next step. The desired value can be set on the aperture ring but without the iris diaphragm in the lens closing. This only happens when a pin in the bayonet is activated by the camera - a result of pressing the shutter release button or depth of field preview lever. TTL metering is done automatically at working aperture but otherwise the diaphragm always remain fully open until the shutter is released.

The auto iris was a great hit right from the beginning and became an indispensible ingredient of later lenses.

Lenses with a meter coupling prong allow open aperture metering with cameras (or finders) equipped with an aperture coupling pin. The aperture ring must be set to f/5.6 when the lens is attached to the camera. Then the ring is set first to the smallest and then to the largest aperture which informs the exposure meter of the maximum aperture.

Lenses with AI-S characteristics are also designed for open aperture metering, but the manual passing of the largest lens aperture to the exposure meter is no longer required on AI cameras and the aperture ring no longer needs to be set to f/5.6 either. Instead a cam engages

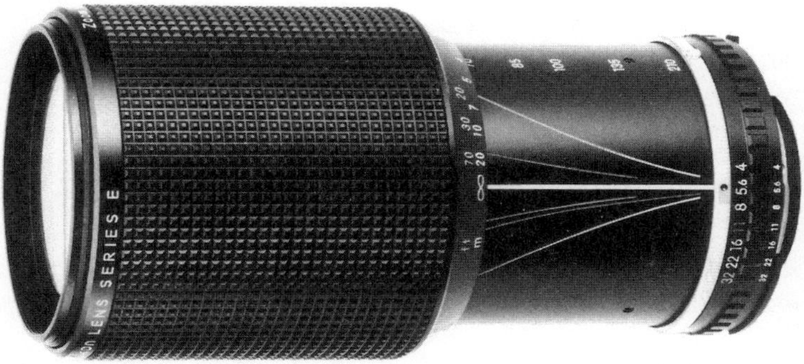

Lenses in the E series are only available without a meter coupling prong.

with an aperture coupling lever. One characteristic of AI lenses is that behind the conventional aperture scale is a second aperture scale with small figures on it. These are read by an optical system and made visible in the viewfinder of suitable cameras. These lenses also feature a meter coupling prong for use with non-AI cameras.

AI-S lenses are also designed to be used with program automatics entailing the automatic switch-over from the normal to the fast program. The camera reads from a raised area on the black ring behind the back lens whether the focal length of the lens is longer than 135mm,in which case it controls the fast version of the program automatic. On AI-S lenses the smallest aperture (highest f/number) on both aperture scales is marked in orange. There is still a meter coupling prong so these lenses can be used on non-AI cameras. One exception was the 50mm,f/1.8lens which, adopted into the normal lens system before the E series, had no driver fork.

E series lenses from the connecting point of view are AI-S lenses without the meter coupling prong. They are designed for use with the Nikon EM, FG and FG-20 and are cheaper than Nikkor lenses. The optical quality of these lenses is not inferior to that of the Nikkors but they are not designed for heavy professional use.

Autofocus lenses without the meter coupling prong are also AI-S type lenses. Manually focused they can be used with AI cameras. The additional autofocusing elements in the bayonet are not in the way.

Peculiarities - specific problems require specific solutions

Apart from a few exceptions the lenses consist of several elements arranged behind each other which are either separate or joined together in groups. The exceptions mentioned are mirror lenses where the mirror is part of the optical system.

All the elements in the lens have two surfaces which could reflect light and thus create flare in the barrel. This in turn could result in the picture appearing flat. The lenses are coated, i.e. microscopically thin layers are vaporized on, to avoid this problem. This method also increases the transmission of light through the lens system. Nikon call their multiple layer system NIC (Nikon Integrated Coating). Not all the elements of a lens are coated in the same way but according to the purpose and material of the element. Of course, a high quality lens element is made of optical glass. But types of glass differ and each has its own refractive index. By combining several types of glass for the elements, chromatic aberration can be corrected. Extra-low dispersion (ED) glass is used primarily for lenses with long focal length to increase their performance.

Focusing alters the distance of the lens to the film. The closer the subject the further away the elements need to be from the film. This is normally achieved by moving the entire lens group forwards with a helicoid thread - which increases the length of the lens. In lenses with internal focusing (IF) only a few internal elements move within the lens barrel, which stays constant in length. In some types of lenses (fast short focal length lenses with retrofocus construction or fast symmetrically-built lenses) focusing by moving all elements equally caused degradation of image quality at close distances. To compensate for this effect Nikon designed lenses whereby close subjects are focused by only moving certain elements in relation to the others.

Protection - for the lens and the picture

If a lens is not in use both front and rear elements should be suitably protected with a cover.

In use the lens should be covered with a lens hood if possible. Not only does this protect the front lens from knocks but it also prevents stray light from entering the lens and causing reflections.

Which Lens for What - fixed focal length or zoom

Both types of lens have their advantages and disadvantages and there is no reason to reject fixed focal length or zooms out of hand. Any good set of equipment consists of lenses from both groups.

The Nikkor 85mm,f/1.4 is a very fast lens. If its full speed capacity is to be used, the depth of field is narrowed so far that you may not even be able to use its widest aperture.

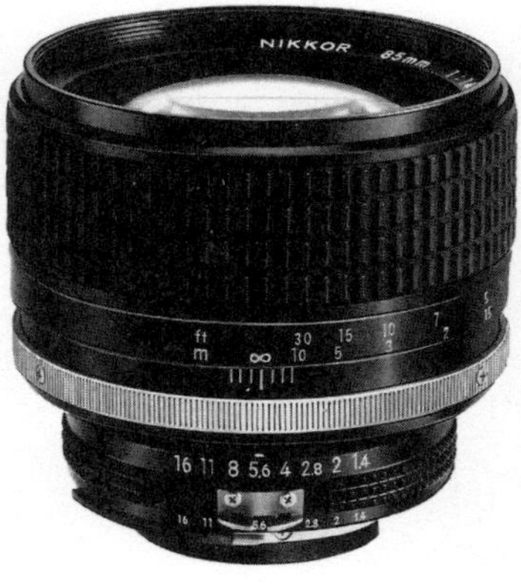

The advantage of fixed focal length...

...is that some focal lengths are just not available as zooms. At full aperture the image quality at the edges of the picture with fixed focal length lenses is, for certain critical subjects such as architecture, superior to that of zooms. The advantage over zooms is clearer where distortion and vignetting are concerned. Fixed focal length lenses are generally also smaller, lighter and have a larger maximum aperture. But focal length is not the only criterion. If you rarely work in low light conditions without flash or tripod, you can content yourself with average speed lenses. And yet, a Nikkor 85mm,f/2 has two more exposure stops for hand-held shots than a 80-200mm,f/4 lens. The depth of field of the faster lens is also shallower with full aperture which means that using selective depth of field is easier.

The disadvantage of fixed focal length lenses is their inflexibility. The image framing must be fixed by selecting a suitable shooting position which inevitably causes an alteration of the perspective. Adjusting the frame finely is also much more difficult than with zooms - a problem when using slide film in particular because you can only change the picture afterwards by making copies.

The foreground frames the main subject and gives it depth, which is missing from the flat two-dimentional shot.

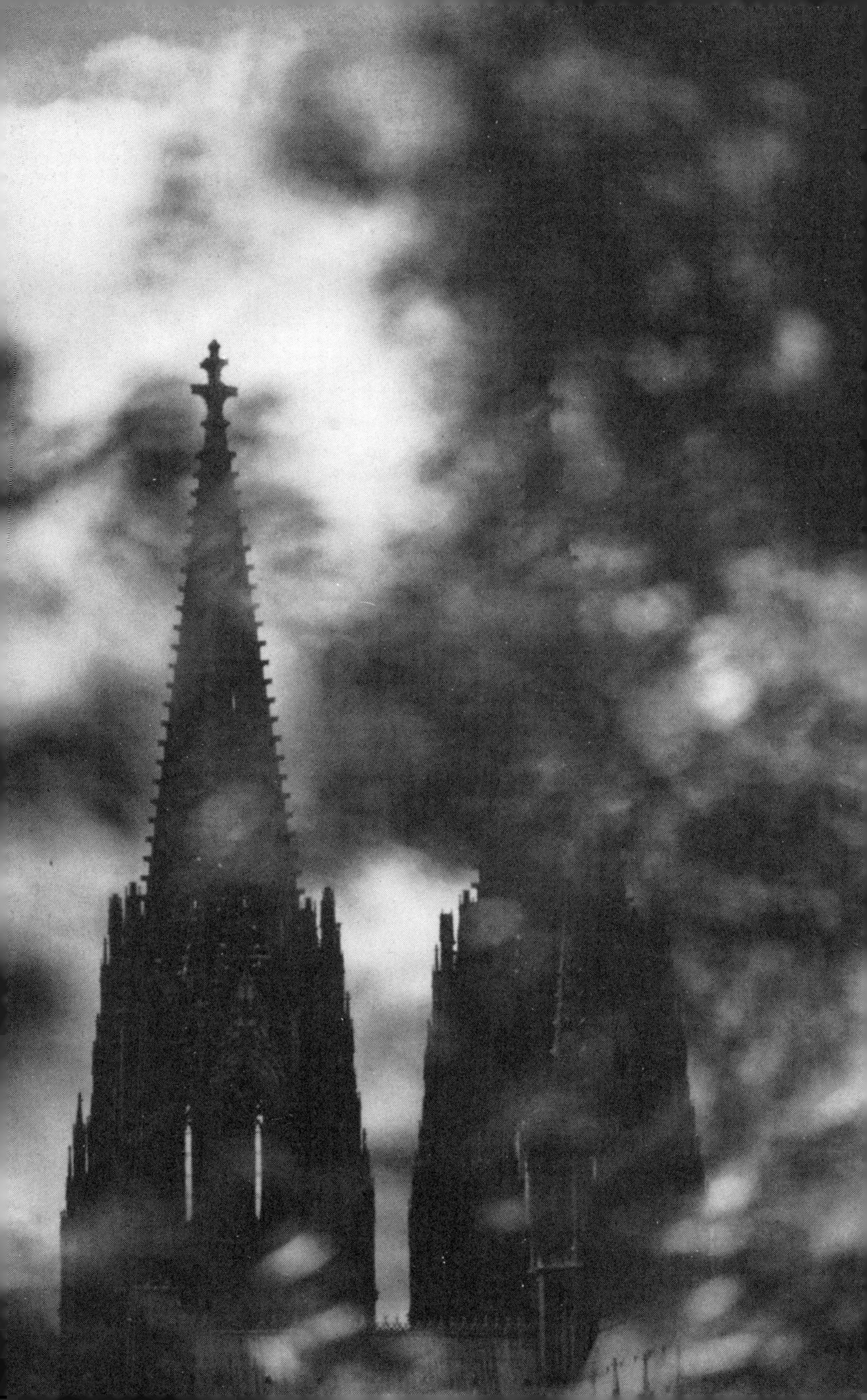

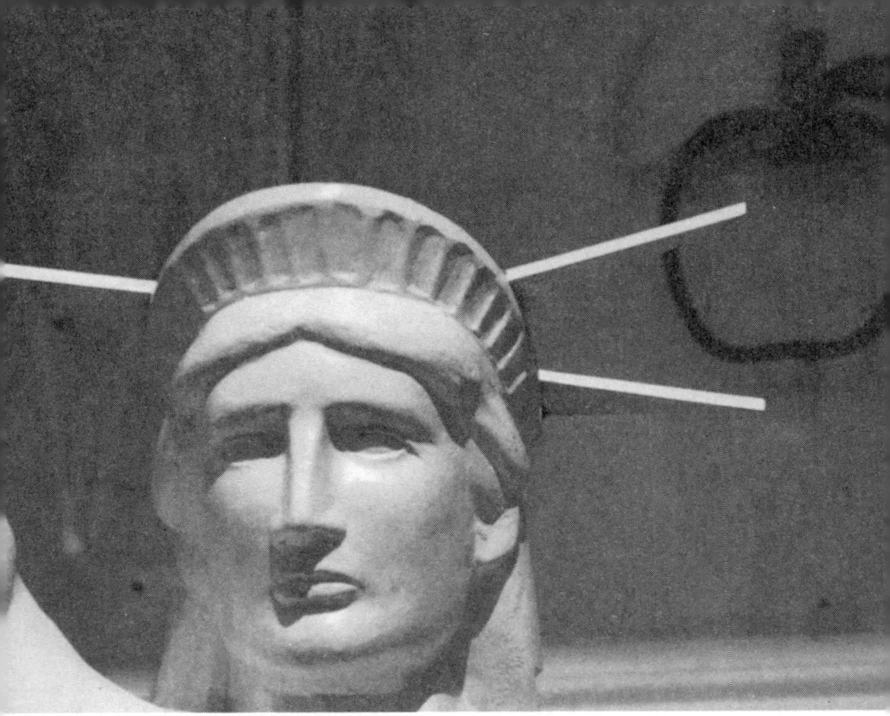

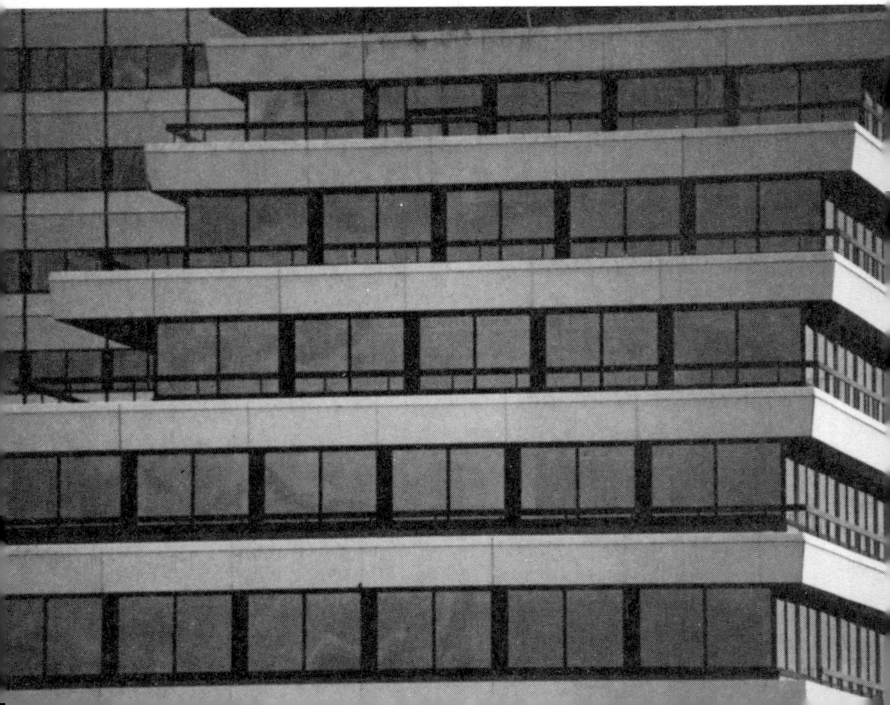

The advantages of zooms...
...are their great flexibility and the fact that only two or three zooms can cover nearly the entire range of focal lengths. Also a quick turn of the focal length ring allows you to eliminate certain unwanted elements from the picture. The reproduction quality of zooms has been greatly improved over the years, although tests prove again and again that fixed focal lengths are superior to zooms as regards to the use of full aperture and full frame emphasis. But in practice many zooms approach fixed focal length lenses in quality and can be recommended even to demanding photographers - especially when these lenses are made by Nikon.

The disadvantage of zooms...
...is that they are quite heavy and generally have smaller maximum apertures than fixed focal length lenses, as well as a tendency towards vignetting when used at full aperture. The smaller maximum apertures can, to a certain extent, be compensated for by using a faster film, but in low light a fixed focal length lens can be hand-held at slower speeds than a zoom.

Top illustration:

A discovery in Cologne: a miniature version of the Statue of Liberty in front of an apple, New York's 'Big Apple' symbol. The automatic program is just right for this snapshot, even if a plus exposure compensation is needed to make sure that the white does not appear too grey.

Bottom illustration:

A slightly raised shooting position means that the large facade comes into the shot without converging lines.

Which Lens for What - normal lenses

Usually a focal length of between 45mm and 55mm is classified as normal for 35mm cameras and for several decades cameras came equipped with a 50mm lens as standard. A change came in the 80s when the cameras started to be sold with zooms around the focal length range of 50mm. These zooms are all-round lenses equally suitable for most subjects. A favourable point is that these normal lenses neither show the steep perspective of wide-angles nor the flattened perspective of telephotos and that the angle of view of a 50mm lens captures only marginally less than the naked eye.

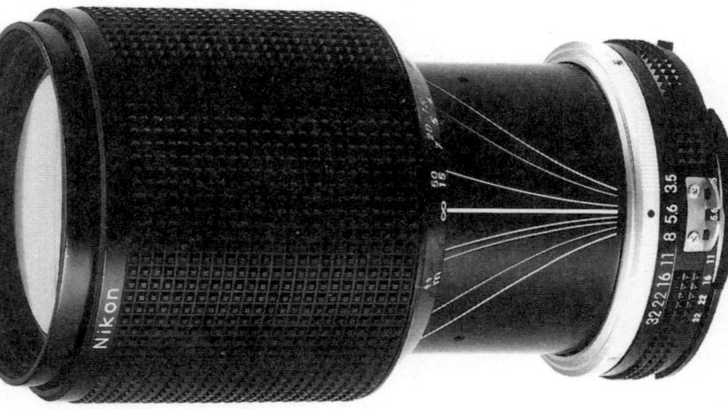

On the Nikkor 50-135mm,f/3.5 zoom focus and distance are selected by means of a slide ring.

A practical advantage is that normal lenses are small, light and quite fast. Although the focal length is generally not the main reason for a particular lens, an f/1.8 or f/1.4 has saved many a shot.

The true giants such as the Nikkor 58mm,f/1.2 Noct are, of course, faster but the question arises whether the greater speed outweighs the higher price.

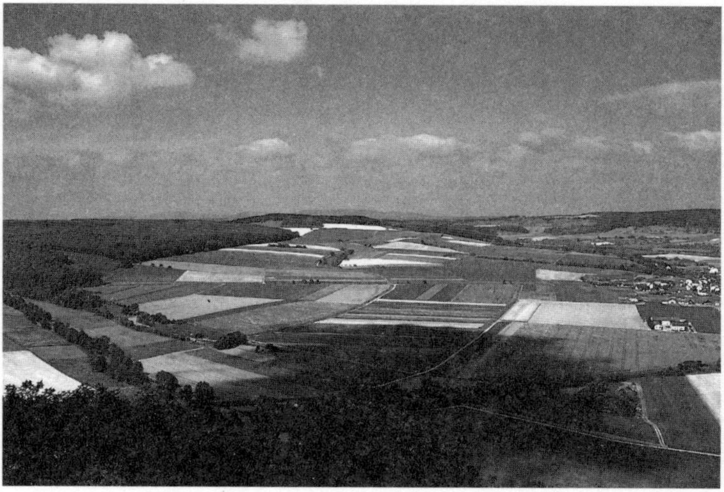

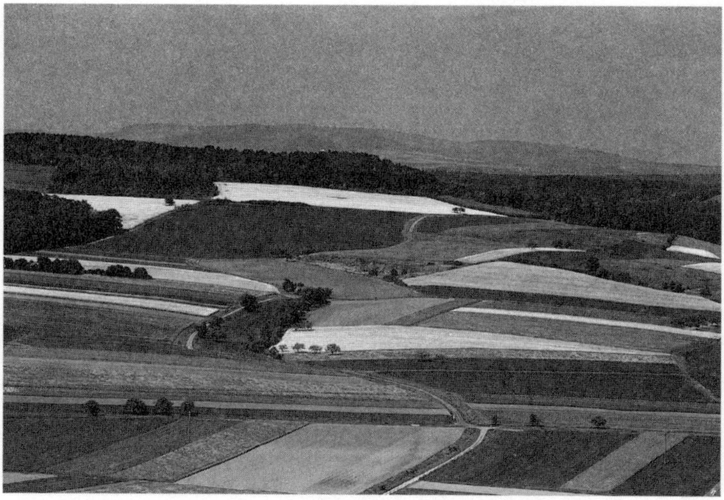

The selection of a suitable image section is fast and convenient with zoom lenses.

Which Lens for What - wide-angles

All lenses with a shorter focal length than a normal lens are classified as wide-angle, although there are differences, too. Down to about 24mm they can be called wide-angles. Lenses of shorter focal length are the ultra wide-angles and fisheyes, with a still shorter focal length, are in a class of their own anyway.

35mm lenses...
...used to be regarded as wide-angles, but these days, partly due to the popularity of compact cameras which usually have a 35mm lens, the 35mm view is accepted as normal. In fact, horizontally it shows what we see with both eyes.

35mm lenses such as the Nikkor 35mm,f/2 and 35-70mm,f/3.3-4.5 can be used for most subjects. Group photographs are captured well with a 35mm lens and snapshots can be taken by using depth of field and dispense with focusing if necessary. Other applications are landscape, panorama views, interiors, interiors with flash, because most flash units illumi-

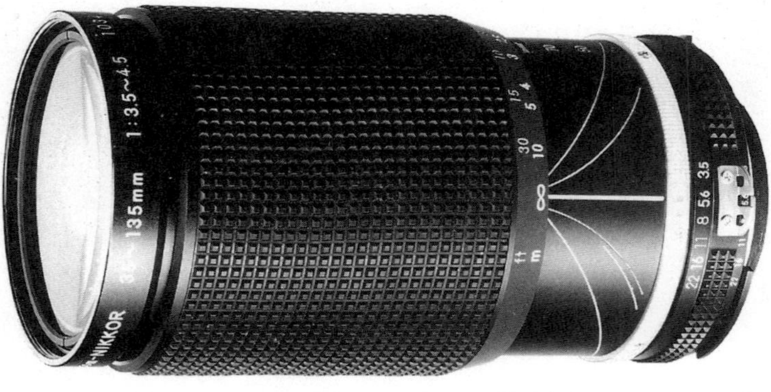

At its shortest focal length the Nikkor 35-135mm, f/3.5-4.5 zoom opens up the wide-angle range. F/3.5 at 35mm focal length isn't exactly breathtaking, but it is only slightly slower than the f/2.8 of many fixed focal length 35mm lenses.

nate the viewing angle of a 35mm lens without additional accessories when the zoom reflector is set to wide-angle or with an wide-angle diffusing screen the brightness is quite even.

28mm lenses...

...have an angle of view of 74° and are still useful when large subjects need to be captured over a long distance, where a panorama view is required. These lenses are less suitable for group photographs or snapshots as either the people are shown very small or - from a short distance - distorted.

The Nikon range includes a 28mm,f/2 and a 28mm, f/2.8 as well as a 28-85mm,f/3.5-4.5 zoom. The AF 24-50mm,f/3.3-4.5 zoom can also be used with AI cameras as it covers both normal and wide-angle ranges.

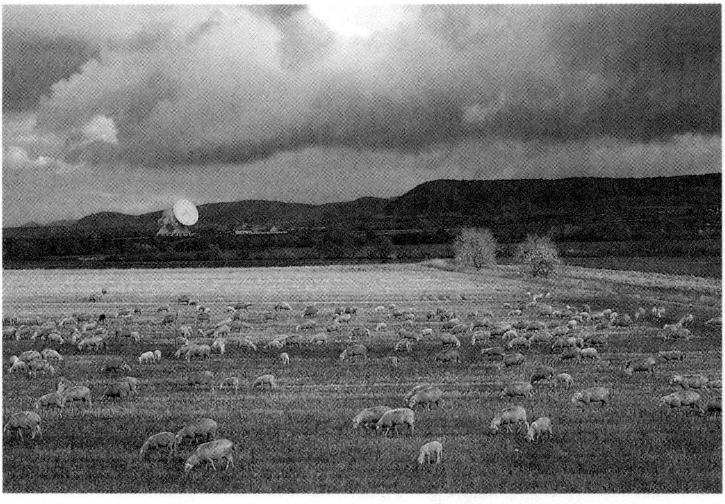

The wide angle of view of short focal length lenses doesn't just have advantages, such as the convincing reproduction of spatial depth. The disadvantage is a huge foreground; however, if it is 'filled' it need no longer be intrusive.

24mm lenses...

...mark the division between wide-angles and ultra wide-angles. The angle of view of 84° can create problems in certain situations; landscape pictures include a great deal of bright sky and occasionally even the sun. This is where the multiple zone metering (AMP) of the Nikon FA has proved itself. Although buildings can be captured completely from a short distance converging lines become very evident, while taken from a greater distance the foreground becomes too prominent.

However, a 24mm lens - whether a fixed focal length such as the Nikkor 24mm,f/2.8 or a zoom - is part of a well-stocked kit as it offers plenty of advantages. It allows grand panoramic views, brings a sense of depth into the picture, and creates some surprising effects. Portraits are perhaps not so flattering but other parts of the anatomy such as legs can be lengthened incredibly!

Which Lens for What - ultra wide-angles

Lenses with a focal length shorter than 24mm clearly belong to the ultra wide-angles. They are represented in the Nikon system by a 20mm, an 18mm, a 15mm and

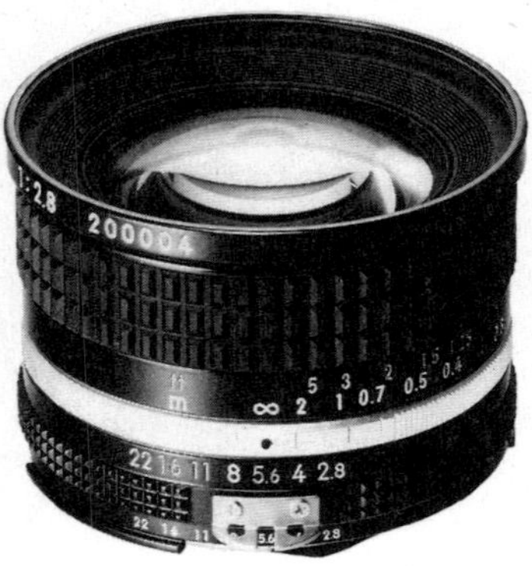

The Nikkor 20mm,f/2.8 is an extremely well-corrected ultra wide-angle lens. The barrel-shaped distortion typical for such lenses (straight lines towards the edge of the shot are pulled outwards) is hardly noticeable.

also a 13mm which is only available to special order. Landscapes, large interiors such as a cathedral, are ideal for these lenses which should really be used with a tripod and a small spirit level in the accessory shoe of the camera.

Which Lens for What - fisheyes

Nikon offers three lenses which allow you to distort the image intentionally. Nikkors 16mm,f/2.8, 8mm,f/2.8 and 6mm,f/2.8 create a barrel-shaped image, i.e. all straight lines not running directly through the centre of the picture converge towards the edge. By using these distortions deliberately, huge picture angles are possible. On the 16mm lens this amounts to 180° diagonally, on the 8mm it is 180° with equidistant projection and the 6mm fisheye has an ultra-wide angle of 220° - literally looking behind the lens. This particular mushroom-shaped lens, however, weighs

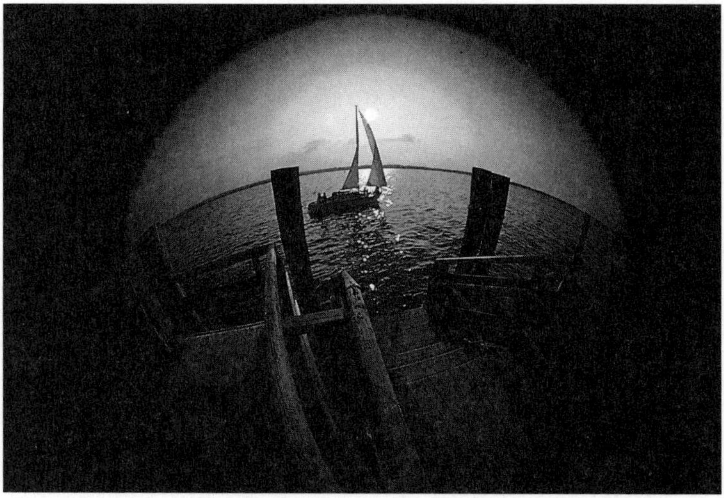

A fisheye pointed downwards shows the world as a sphere - the straight line of the horizon is distinctly bent downwards.

more than 5kg and is only available to special order so it is hardly practical for normal photography. Of the two other fisheyes the 16mm version is more useful as it gives you full frame pictures whereas the 8mm only produces a circular image of 23mm on a 24x36mm frame. Close interiors, a landscape under a grey overcast sky, abstract rock formations or cars shot from a ground level viewpoint are all subjects that can be recorded in an entirely new light when seen with a fisheye.

Which Lens for What - telephotos

The classification "telephoto" covers all lenses with a focal length longer than 50mm.

Portrait lenses...
...cover the focal lengths from 85mm to 135mm because they allow you to take perfect pictures of a face or portrait. The distance to the subject is not too small and the perspective which renders a face flat in the picture is not too pronounced. In addition, the depth of field at full aperture is still shallow enough to allow the subject to be clearly defined against a blurred background. These lenses are also very suitable for landscape or nature photography as detail can be separated well from the whole.

A typical portrait lens is the Nikkor 85mm,f/2 as is the Nikkor 105mm,f/18. A focal length of 135mm is almost too long for portraiture. Lenses like the Nikkor 135mm,f/2.8 are useful for reportage and snapshot purposes as they can be used from a medium distance and still give a frame-filling picture. The small angle of view cuts out any unwanted surroundings. The shallow depth of field is a focusing advantage in connection with full aperture and subject and background are clearly separated.

Conventional telephotos...

...from 200mm to 300mm are not only useful when capturing a subject over a great distance - a castle on a mountain across a valley, for example. Over medium distances the Nikkor 200mm,f/4 or zoom lenses 80-200mm,f/4 and 50-300mm,f/4.5 fill the frame even with small subjects.

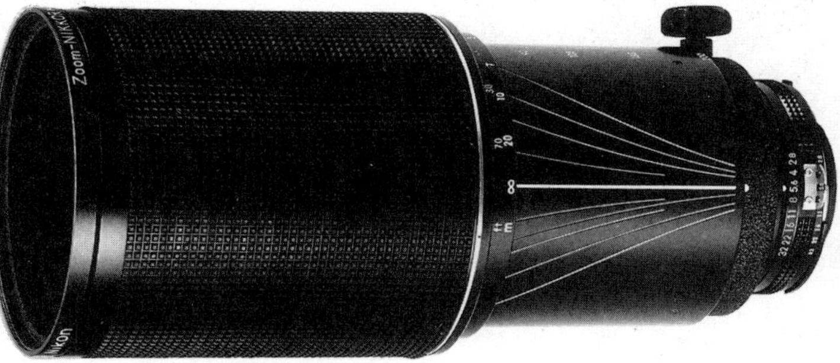

80-200mm zooms are the tele zooms. They offer all the most important telephoto focal lengths in one go. The Nikkor 80-200mm,f/2.8 is a fast example of this group.

Telephotos are often used for sports, nature or reportage photography but their ability optically to compress a subject like a mountain range makes them useful for many other applications as well.

Which Lens for What - super telephotos

These monsters are special purpose lenses rarely used in everyday photography. With a weight of over 6kg for the Nikkor 600mm,f/4 ED-IF or a length of 40cm for a 180-600mm zoom these lenses are intended for special tasks and only available on special order. They are certainly too large, too heavy and - most importantly - too expensive for the amateur photographer.

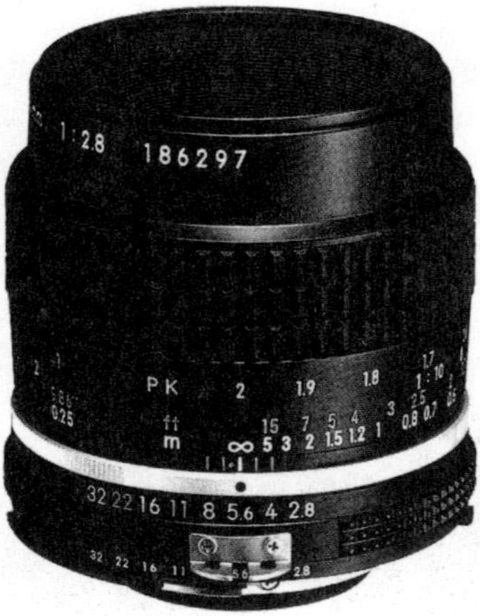

The 55mm,f/2.8 micro Nikkor offers a largest reproduction ratio of 1:2 without additional equipment. This means that the subject is reproduced at half its actual size. If you're interested in macro photography, you won't be able to do without such a lens.

Which Lens for What - special purpose lenses

Special purpose lenses are generally usable wherever other lenses of the same focal length are used. They cost more than the ordinary form and should only be bought if the specific purpose warrants it.

Macro lenses...

...Nikon calls them Micro. They are designed for close-up work and provide a reproduction ratio of 1:2 (half lifesize) and 1:1. Even more special is the Nikkor 200mm,f/4 Micro, a true macro telephoto which can pull in the subject over a distance of 50cm at a reproduction ratio of 1:2.

PC Nikkors...

...35mm,f/2.8 and 28mm,f/3.5 can only be used with working aperture metering as these perspective control (PC) lenses can be shifted upwards, downwards and sideways, pushing undesirable foreground out of the picture while pulling in the upper part of a building, for example. An auto iris can therefore not be operated mechanically from the camera.

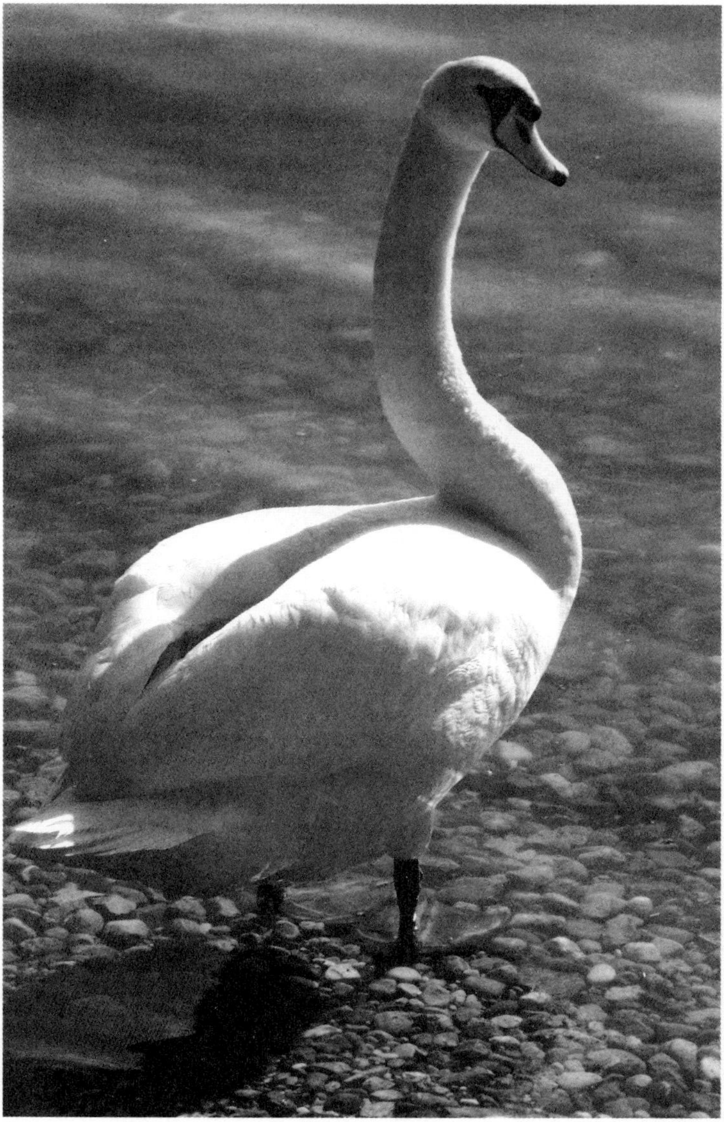

A telephoto lens enables the photographer to take shots of animals without disturbing them - and without the risk of being pecked by a swan!

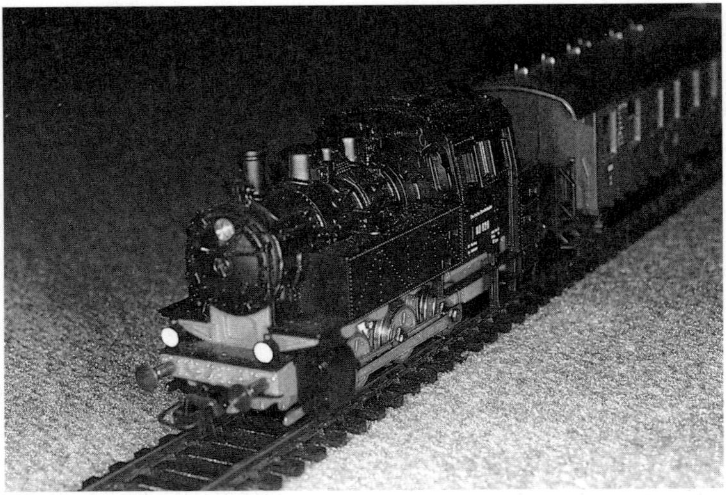

Macro lenses open up the world of small things and give new appeal to old toys

Not only do these lenses push out unwanted items from the picture without changing position they can also be used to take a stereo effect picture by making two exposures with a shift to the left and then to the right. Panoramic views can also be created by joining two exposures together.

Which Lens for What - teleconverters

Teleconverters are not really lenses but they extend the focal length when attached between lens and camera. A 2x extender doubles the focal length with a loss of two aperture stops. A 1.4x converter provides a 1.4 increase in focal length with a reduction of 1 stop.

There is a wide range of converters in the Nikon system, not equally suitable for all lenses, however.

Models TC-14A, TC-14B and TC-16A increase the focal

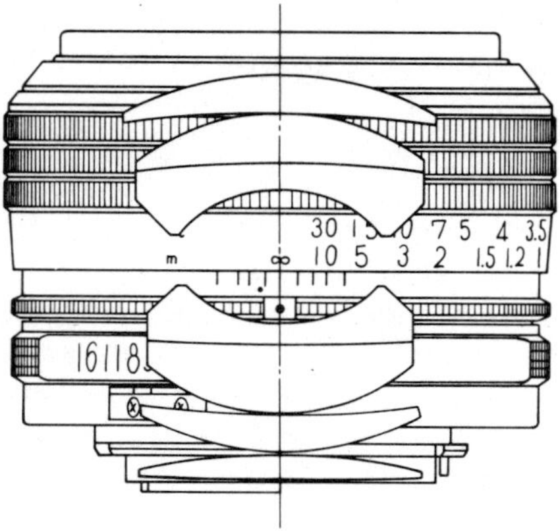

Fast lenses require sophisticated production techniques. Their price is correspondingly high and only worth paying if you frequently need fast lenses.

length by 1.4 times, TC-201 and TC-301 double it. Roughly speaking A type converters are suitable for focal lengths up to 200mm, B type converters and the TC-301 are for longer focal lengths.

Terminology - explanation in connection with lenses

The speed...

...represents the maximum aperture of a lens and stands for the ratio of the entrance pupil - the hole in the aperture as seen through the front element - to the focal length. This enables comparisons of speed between lenses of different focal lengths to be made directly. At f/8 the entrance pupil fits into the focal length eight times and the same amount of light reaches the film, no matter what focal length lens is used. The speed is determined by the largest aperture.

The larger the maximum aperture the faster the speed of the lens, the brighter the viewfinder image, the shallower the possible depth of field and the dimmer the light in which exposures can be made without the need for a flash or tripod. But a shallow depth of field can have a negative effect as only a part of the subject is in focus. The faster the speed the more expensive the lens and if the largest aperture is only rarely used a lot of money can be wasted.

The macro setting...

...on many zoom lenses is an extra. A greater reproduction ratio of 1:4 allows you to capture a butterfly or a pretty flower in passing. When stopped down - perhaps to f/8 or f/11- the lens gives good results. A small tripod could reduce or prevent the danger of camera shake. However, true macro photographers are better served with a Micro Nikkor or bellows.

The perspective...

...is not dependent on the lens but on the shooting position. The change from standing to kneeling or a tiny step to the left or right alters the perspective but not the focal length. When changing the focal length (and so the angle of view) and thus the position - e.g. closer with a wide-angle, further away with a telephoto - the focal length affects the perspective after all, but only indirectly.

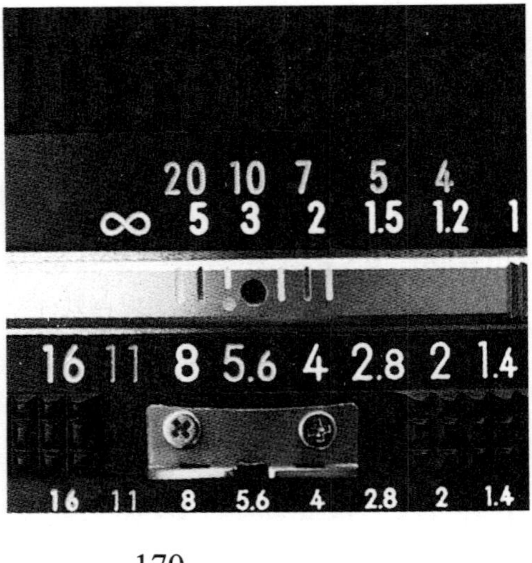

The coloured layout of the focus control scale makes it possible to determine an extension of the area of sharpness on certain lenses, and to determine focusing distances. With the right aperture/distance combination it is possible to take sharp photographs without focusing.

The depth of field...
...also depends on the lens. The shorter the focal length the greater the extent of the depth of field.

The depth of field scale...
...of Nikkor lenses is easy to use. To the left and right of the index the aperture scale appears as a mirror image. The larger apertures are closer to the index than the smaller apertures. When you set the distance on the index you can see from the two equal aperture values the extent of the depth of field with the set aperture and distance. Coloured markings simplify the procedure.

The snapshot setting...
...is based on the large depth of field with short focal lengths and small apertures. You select the aperture and distance which gives the required depth of field for your subject. You can read these off the depth of field scale on the lens. If you take a picture of a subject within the depth of field there is no need to focus and you are as quick, if not quicker, than an AF camera user.

Converging lines...
...occur when parallel lines run away from the direction of the camera. In the picture they run towards each other, away from the camera position. This effect is usually noticed with architectural photography as converging lines appear when a building is photographed with a camera held at an angle to it to get it all in. Even when the camera is held level, converging lines may occur - for example, railway tracks or a road. PC lenses allow you to avoid converging lines in architectural photography. However, converging lines can also increase the effect of a picture.

Flash - Added Light

The operating manuals of the cameras described in this book show small diagrams which give the shutter speeds for the different flash bulbs. This is more out of courtesy to those photographers who value the long burning time - and the option of using fast shutter speeds with flash - of such flash bulbs even today. Of greater importance, however, are electronic flash units offered by Nikon and independent manufacturers.

When Nikon in 1976 entered autofocus technology with its F-501 the first new generation flash unit was introduced at the same time which allowed AF cameras to focus even in the dark by using an AF illuminator. These flash units are the automatic TTL type but can also be used as computer flashes and are therefore also usable with older cameras - if you are not actually using a Nikon AF camera in conjunction with one of the oldies mentioned in this book, AF flash units are of no interest to you. After all, you would be paying for output you do not need. But the Nikon system features a number of interesting flash units apart from the AF units.

Flash units SB-16B and hammerheads SB-11and SB-14 (connectable to the camera's TTL control by TTL Remote Cord SC-23) are suitable for the FE2 and FA cameras. Without the remote cord both hammerhead flash units can be used as normal computer flash on older cameras such as the Nikon F, Nikkormat FT2, Nikkormat EL and Nikon FM. This requires Sensor Remote Cord SC-13 and Sensor Unit SU-2. If the hammerhead flash units are too large and heavy, a non-system unit such the Vivitar 283 offers greater convenience with the same output.

Nikon SB-16B - two automatic flash heads

Like many flash units the Nikon SB-16B is connected to the camera by the accessory shoe which is not very desirable as the light falls on the subject from the front creating heavy shadows behind it. Direct light cannot add depth to the subject and subsequently it appears quite flat.

This can be remedied by using a tilting flash reflector as featured by the Nikon SB-16B. The large reflector can be tilted up to 90° in five click-stops, in addition it can be rotated by 90° to the right and by 180° to the left (i.e. backwards) allowing you to beam the harsh flash light to the subject via a reflecting surface making it softer. Obviously the reflecting surface must not be too far away or the flash will lose power on the way. When using a colour slide film such as Ektachrome 100 or Kodachrome 200 the reflecting surface should be white so not to transfer any colouring to the subject. A LumiQuest reflector can be attached to the flash unit with Velcro tape and it provides light whenever and wherever. Indirect light is always preferable to direct light but there could be problems with portraits. If the light comes from above, unattractive shadows will appear under eyebrows, nose and chin of the subject. The Nikon SB-16B has a static second reflector to avoid this problem.

The angle of coverage of the main flash head is variable to different viewing angles - 28mm, 35mm, 50mm and 85mm - whereby the guide number will change, of course. When set to 35mm with an ISO 100 film the metre guide number will be 32.

When TTL controlled the camera automatically switches off the flash at the right moment. When not used with TTL control or if the film speed is outside the range of ISO 25/15° to ISO 400/27° suitable for TTL there are two computer apertures available. They are separated by two aperture stops and according to film

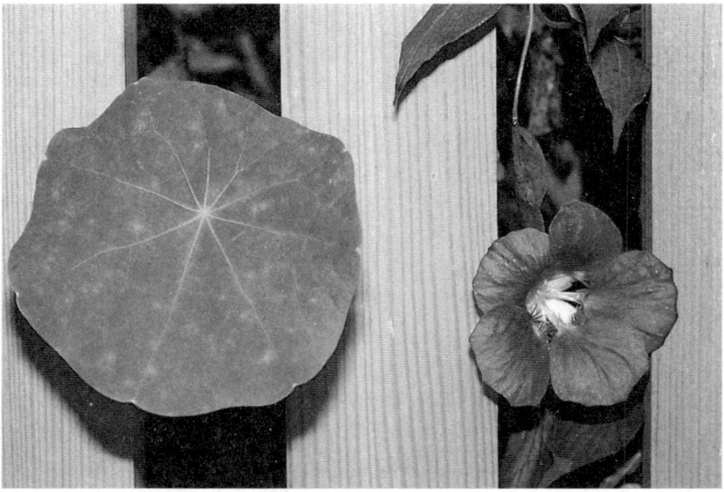

A flashgun can be useful even outside. TTL flash control allows free aperture selection, which in turn allows the selection of a certain depth of field.

speed are greater or smaller - in the case of ISO 100/21° it is f/4 and f/8. Naturally the flash can also be used with the guide number calculation which always provides the full flash energy. A variation of manual control is the MD mode. The flash output is the same from flash to flash - $^{1}/_{16}$ of the full power which corresponds to a guide number of 8. This reduction allows you to use flash even with motorized series - although longer series are only possible over short distances. The number of times the flash lights up depends on the subject, the background and the age of the four 1.5V batteries powering the flash.

Nikon SB-11 and SB-14 - high-power, high-performance

Hammerhead flash units Nikon SB-11(guide number 36 for ISO 100/21°) and SB-14 are designed for photographers using flash very often. The already heavy

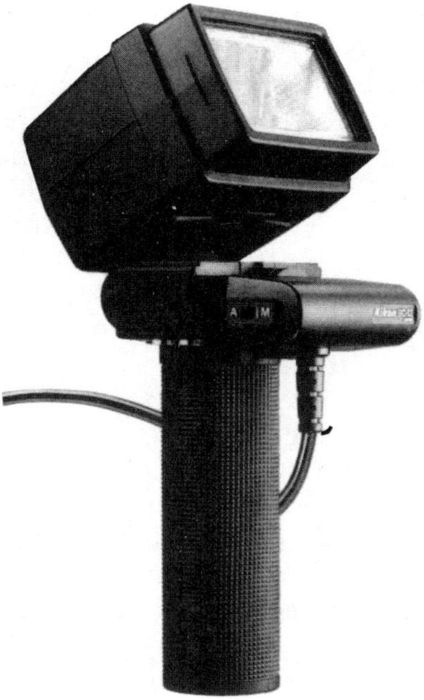

The SB-14 is a hammerhead flash designed for professional use. Important features are high flash capacity and fast recycling time.

Nikon SB-11accommodates its eight 1.5V AA batteries in the handle whereas the SB-14 requires an separate power pack with six 1.5V C-type batteries.

The flash head of the SB-11can be tilted, the head of the SB-14 can rotate as well, making indirect illumination of the subject easy.

The TTL Remote Cord SC-23 allows both flash units to be controlled by automatic TTL of a suitably equipped Nikon camera.

When using different cameras both flash units can be used as full computer flashes. Sensor Unit SU-2 is fastened to the flash unit connected to the camera by a normal sync cable. This applies primarily to the Nikon F which has no conventional accessory shoe. In this case the sensor is rather far away from the lens and in the worst situation it can happen that the lens views something different from the flash sensor - the flash exposure does not correspond to the subject.

To avoid trouble the sensor can be removed from the flash unit and Sensor Cord SC-13 used instead of the sync cable. One end of the cord is plugged into the normal sensor socket on the flash while the other end is connected to the accessory shoe of the camera transferring the flash signal from the hot shoe to the flash unit. This second plug of the SC-13 is the same as the sensor plug of the SB-11 and SB-14. That means that the sensor can be connected to the second plug of the SC-13 which is close above the lens.

The consecutive f/numbers for computer working apertures can be set on the Sensor Unit SU-2 - in the case of an ISO 100/21° film they are f/4, f/5.6 and f/8.

These large flash units also allow manual control by guide number calculation which, in the case of the SB-14 gives a reach of 18m, when a film such as Ektachrome 100 is loaded and the lens is set to f/2.

Nikon's current range of flashguns, e.g. the SB-24, are compatible, to a certain degree, with all the cameras mentioned in this book.

Terminology - a few explanations regarding flash units

The computer flash...

...features a sensor receiving and metering the light reflected from the subject. When the light is sufficient to expose the film correctly the computer flash switches off - this might be after $^1/_{50000}$ sec or after $^1/_{1000}$ sec. In order for the film to be exposed correctly you also set the lens to the right f/number for which the flash meters the exposure. Simple flash units provide one such computer flash aperture while others can be used with several different apertures which allows a certain amount of freedom when using depth of field to compose the picture.

With the relevant accessories, several flashguns can be controlled from the camera, with flash exposure metering taking place in the camera. However, as there are no auxiliary lights, the use of several small flashguns is not always to be recommended because the effect of light and shade can't be judged before the exposure is made

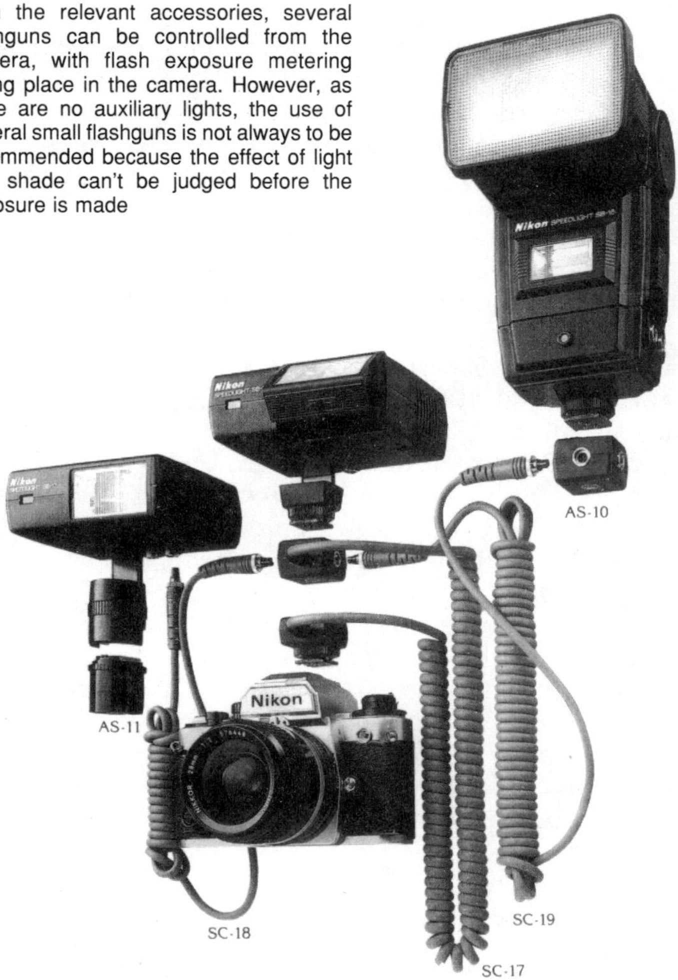

Computer apertures depend on the film speed. Available apertures for the film speed and also the reach of the flash with different apertures is indicated on the calculator of the flash unit.

The use of a separate flash...

...is required in order to illuminate the subject from the side or to simulate the light of the morning sun. The flash unit must be separated from the camera and connected by a long sync cable to the flash socket. The guide number calculation must take into account the actual distance of flash to subject.

The guide number...

...gives the output of the flash unit. Today it usually refers to a film speed of ISO 100/21° and the distance in metres. The relationship between guide number, flash aperture and distance is represented by the guide number formula.

flash aperture = guide number : distance

When you reverse the formula you can find out how far a flash unit with known guide number will reach at a specific aperture:

Distance = guide number : aperture.

Both formulae are not applicable every time, however. When shooting in a large dark room or outside at night, part of the light is lost that in smaller rooms is reflected from the ceiling, walls, bright curtains and furniture. Therefore open the aperture by 1 stop or more when using the flash outside or don't exploit the calculated maximum range.

The sync speed...

...is the shutter speed at which the first blind reveals the film area while the second blind has not yet started to close it again. At that moment the brief light from the flash is able to reach the whole film area.

At faster shutter speeds the second blind closes the film window while the flash is still lit. The result is that part of the film is blanked off and can be seen in the picture as a black strip.

Films - The Stuff of Pictures

When buying a camera many photographers first ask about the types of lenses available. The second question is about the right type of film to use. If you want to use your SLR camera to transform the subject at its best don't simply ask for "colour film".

The ideal film for all situations and subjects does not exist. But search around a little and you will find the right film for your needs. There are two types of film and four ranges of film speed which all have many advantages but also a few disadvantages.

The film speed range - how much is enough?

Each film requires a certain amount of light to reproduce a picture correctly. The amount a particular film requires is indicated as the film speed.

The two extremes are:

Low-speed films which are noticeable for their extremely high sharpness and fine grain. Typical low-speed films are the negative film Ektar 25 and the slide film Kodachrome 25, the latter's leading position for many years being challenged by films such as Ektachrome 50 HC.

These films require a lot of light. If this is not taken into account many a shot can be lost because of blurring due to camera shake. In addition you need an excellent system (tripod-film-enlarger/projector) to do justice to the high quality of these films.

The high-speed films...

...at the other end of the range need only a little light. In some cases it is even possible to dispense with flash altogether (typical example is Ektapress Gold 1600).

Care is required when using these films as in bright surroundings they need large f/numbers giving large depth of field - unless a camera like the FM2, FE2 or FA is used and the $^{1}/_{4000}$ sec available provides an effective light barrier.

The grain of these films is also not fine enough to be suitable for all subjects.

Both low and high-speed films therefore are special purpose films for particular situations.

For general photography there remain two films of medium speed; normal and fast films.

Normal films...

...nowadays have a speed of ISO 100/21°, ISO 160/23° or ISO 200/24°, while ISO 125 and 160 films are still outsiders.

Films of ISO 100/21° are almost always right. Particularly suitable for daylight they also give good results at dawn or dusk as long as camera shake can be avoided. With additional light from a flash or a photographic lamp the ISO 100 film also provides the right material for use at night or in dark interiors.

The colours appear true - although each brand renders the colours a little differently. If you prefer rather softer colours choose Ektachrome 100 from Kodak, for rich colours Ektachrome 100 HC might be more suitable. Sharpness and contrast are good and the grain is satisfactory as well. The latter is one of the reasons why ISO 100 films can be used not only from early to late, winter or summer, but also for all distances from far to close-up (macro). Fine detail is not obscured by grain.

ISO 200 films can be classified in a similar way. Although critical subjects show a little more grain, generally speaking the graininess of these films normally present no problems and they also can be called all-round films.

High-speed films...

...with a speed of ISO 400/27° or ISO 1000/31° are more suitable for dull days, dawn and dusk, interiors with and without flash. ISO 400 films are also right for slow lenses such as the Nikkor 100-300,f/5.6; they should be used primarily within the normal distance range, though. For macro photography a slower film could be more suitable if conditions allow it.

Regarding the grain, ISO 400 films are inferior to ISO 100 and 200 films, although the new ISO 400 films have a much finer grain than those of a few years ago. Black-and-white films with a speed of ISO 400/27° especially are excellent as regards grain.

This development was made possible through the arrival of new technologies in the production of light-sensitive films and Kodak's T crystals are one example.

The amateur photographer can use ISO 100, 200 and 400 films for the majority of his work. When the speeds of these films are exhausted, slower films with highest contour sharpness and faster films turning night into day, photographically speaking, are offered by the major film manufacturers.

Types of film - colour or tones of grey? Album or projection?

The first decision the film buyer needs to make is choosing between colour and black-and-white film followed by the decision between negative or transparency. Both factors can be combined to give 4 choices:

- colour transparency
- colour negative
- black-and-white negative
- black-and-white transparency

Black-and-white transparency films are hardly ever available today and those that are still around can be regarded as special purpose films. The other three film types apply to amateur photography equally well.

The black-and-white film...

...is again gaining a great following after having been neglected in favour of colour films by amateurs since the 60s.

The newest black-and-white films such as one of the Kodak T-Max series can hardly be improved upon as regards their reproduction capability. More improvements are certain to be made which shows that conventional film is still superior to electronic still video recording.

Fine grain and high resolution allow sharp reproduction of even the minutest structures. The ISO 100 films show hardly any grain even when enlarged to a great size and the higher speed films such as T-Max 400 or T-Max P3200 (which can be exposed like an ISO 400/27° or ISO 6400/39° film) give such excellent results even when greatly enlarged.

Indeed, new emulsion technologies have made ISO 400 black-and-white films so good that many photographers use them all the time and only resort to ISO 100 films for macro photography of detailed subjects.

It is still recommended to expose for a little longer and develop for a little shorter in order to achieve pictures with a good tone reproduction. When metering the exposure direct the camera towards the darker parts of the subject. The clear definition of the central metering zone enables you to meter the desired subject part accurately.

You will find out how to develop these films to produce negatives by experimenting a little as you will have to process most black-and-white films yourself.

Most laboratories that used to deal with black-and-white films have disappeared nowadays and processing the films at home is the only option - probably the better option anyway.

Processing a film is not difficult. For example, Kodak offer ready mixed developing solutions for their T-Max films. Enlargers for the negative-positive process are not too expensive and some modular units can be adapted to colour photography at a later date. But a simple black-and-white version is sufficient. You also need vessels for developing, rinsing and fixing the pictures, some forceps for transferring the pictures from one dish to another, graduated cylinders and a thermometer to measure out the chemicals and warm them to the correct temperature.

There is no particular skill required to process your own black-and-white films.

Three points speak in favour of a home-based darkroom; you can determine exactly the section of the picture when enlarging - even deviating from the not always optimal ratio of 2:3 of a 35mm film.

You can optimize the picture by dodging an under-exposed shot or using masks. And in your own laboratory you can experiment to your heart's content.

Colour negative films...

...are by far the most popular film material for the amateur photographer. Here, too, there are decisions to be made.

Choose a normal film such as Kodacolor Gold 100, when you want prints of the whole negative which you can then store in a photo album or hang on the wall and also when you know that your film will remain in the camera for some time. These films are good-natured products where exposure latitude is concerned.

In connection with a Nikon camera with TTL metering the exposure latitude of the film is not as important as with compact cameras. But even with a Nikon FT2 or FA it is comforting to know that over or under exposure within two aperture stops will not immediately lead to ruined pictures. Even if the emergency shutter speed of $^1/_{250}$ sec needs to be applied with these cameras the exposure latitude is indeed a very welcome feature of negative films.

As these films can be regarded as all round films, suitable for simple compact cameras as well as sophisticated SLRs the film speeds are graded to accommodate all camera types.

An ISO 100 film such as the Kodacolor Gold 100 is suitable for any situation - from A for Architecture to L for Landscape, P for Portrait and Z for Zebras in the zoo.

An ISO 200 film is especially suitable for landscapes, snapshots and indoor portraits and can be regarded as universal material when slow zooms such as the excellent Nikkor 80-200mm,f/4 are used.

In the same situation an ISO 400 film would need a shutter speed faster by 1-stop. This film is preferable when shooting without a tripod in low light (i.e. outside at dusk or indoors), or with flash when the output of the unit used must reach a long way.

If necessary the computer control of the flash unit cannot be used as the higher film speed usually results in smaller apertures and greater depths of field.

For very big enlargements, sectional enlargements or fine structures high performance films such as those of the Kodak Ektar series are the right choice. But in order to do justice to the high quality of these films the entire equipment from film to lens and exposure meter right through to the enlarger must be right.

Regarding exposure meters, those fitted to Nikon cameras should present no problems. The ISO 25/15° setting for the Ektar 25 is available as is ISO 125/22° for the medium speed Ektar 125.

High speed films such as the Ektar 1000 are really special purpose films for low light conditions in the area of colour negatives as well - the low light may consist of daylight mixed with normal light bulbs or fluorescent lighting.

Colour negative films as well as black-and-white films can give you the incentive to extend your hobbyto include the work in your own darkroom once the shots are taken.

One fact true for all pictures is that the bigger the better.

Colour transparency films...

...or slide films - apart from one exception - can be developed at home but this is not recommended. It is better to use a professional laboratory which can process the film in under two hours.

The exception mentioned is Kodachrome films as their special design requires these to be processed only in Kodak laboratories. Principally these films are black-and-white films which are coloured during processing. Very thin layers are possible which have a positive effect on the sharpness performance of these films. Kodachrome films are available at speeds of ISO 25/25°, ISO 64/19° and ISO 200/24° while Ektachrome films for E-6 processing are available at speeds of ISO 50/18°, ISO 100/21°, ISO 200/24° and ISO 400/27°. Also included in this range is a film with a variable speed of between ISO 800/30° and ISO 3200/36°. Some films like the above-mentioned film with variable speed are only available as professional films, others feature a professional version in conjunction with an amateur film.

Professional films are no better than others - they are just more suitable for professional requirements. For example, there will be no variation between films of the same batch when the same subject is used for several films.

What value have professional films for the amateur? These films must be treated professionally, i.e. stored in a cool place, used rapidly and developed as soon after exposure as possible.

There is no reason for the amateur to use professional films except when they are on special offer or used in semi-professional situations.

Accessories - Small Things keep you Interested

A camera, a few lenses and you can record a journey around the world. And the addition of a flash unit and a motor drive makes things easier, quicker and safer. What else do you need? Well - a tripod and a few filters are useful even for everyday photography; and cable releases, bellows and a copy stand if you are interested in macro photography. Nikon offers a wide range of photographic accessories.

Automatic Bellows - easier close-ups

Micro Nikkor lenses are excellent for close-up photography. If you want to use reproduction ratios beyond 1:1,however, or to copy and alter slides then sooner or later you will need a bellows focusing attachment.

The Nikon Bellows Focusing Attachments are fitted between the camera body and lens and serve as the most versatile single attachments for close-ups or macrophotography. Accepting virtually all the Nikkor lenses, the attachments provide a wide range of magnification ratios. They may be used on a tripod or with the copy stand.

Filter Systems - for better as well as different pictures

Filters can be divided into two groups. Some are used to optimize the picture as the lens sees it. Others allow you to alter the subject during exposure and to introduce other elements which are not really there.

Filters of the first group are the UV and skylight filters which filter out the excessive UV rays in the light and prevent the picture having a blue cast. The polarizing filter is also a utility filter as it provides clearer and richer colours and reduces the glare from non-metallic surfaces. The reflections of glass windows and water can sometimes be partially or completely eliminated by these filters. The effect of polarizing filters is influenced by the angle between the optical axis and the light source, it is therefore prudent to observe the viewfinder image carefully.

Blue conversion filters alter the colour of artificial light on a daylight film while an amber conversion filter adjusts the daylight for artificial light films.

Colour filters are also important for black-and-white photography as they can improve the contrasts.

On the border between utility and creative filters are the graduated filters. Graduated neutral density filters balance the contrast, e.g. between bright sky and a dark landscape - and colour graduated filters intensify the colours for the picture. A milky grey sky can be given a more natural blue colour, or an emerald green, tobacco brown or one of many other colourings.

Apart from these graduated filters there are also many different effect filters; soft focus filters diffuse portraits or add haze to a landscape; starburst filters add magical lights to night photography. Multiple prism filters multiply the subject several times in one picture and blurring filters create the illusion of movement.

All the filters mentioned and many more are featured in the Cokin range. Also included are lens attachments such as close-up lenses. The advantage of such a filter system is that thanks to a clever adapter system all filters fit all lenses. You only make a single decision between using size "A" for almost any 35mm lenses or "P" for medium format lenses and KB lenses with a large filter thread (giant telephotos or wide-angles). In order to change a filter simply slide the almost square filter in the two grooves in the holder. Several filters fit into one Cokin holder allowing you two combine special effects quickly.

Another advantage of the Cokin filter system is that stray-light filters can be attached - not only important when shooting in low light conditions but also when there is none available with a lens bought secondhand.

(See *Cokin Filter System for Photo and Video*-Hove Foto Books).

Remote Shutter Release - to eliminate blur

The simplest form of remote release is the cable release which is simply screwed into the socket of the shutter release button, or - in the case of older Nikon cameras - around the shutter release button.

A cable release is important when using a tripod to avoid any vibration caused by the manual pressing of the shutter button.

Anti-cold Battery Holder - power in the cold

The Nikon Anti-cold Battery Holder DB-2 accepts two 1.5V AA batteries and is connected to the battery chamber of the camera by a cable. The camera must be able to accept this type of battery.

Copy Stand - hobby within a hobby

Copying forms a special part of photography as a hobby.

A copy stand allows you to make copies of flat originals such a newspapers, illustrations, photographs, stamps, coins etc. Various types of light bulbs can be attached such as fluorescent, halogen or opaque bulbs. For slide copying special brackets hold colour mixing heads which can be used to alter the colour in the picture. A camera with a bellows can also be attached for close-up work.

Tripods - a firm stand

Although the lens had been focused correctly many photographs appear blurred. Generally the rule of thumb can be applied to assess the danger of camera shake; slowest shutter speed for hand-held exposures equals one divided by the focal length in mm.

When the shutter speed approaches or drops belows that value the camera can be supported by a small tripod or stabilizer which can be folded up neatly to fit into your bag.

For slower shutter speeds or when the camera is equipped with a heavy zoom or telephoto plus a motor drive a sturdy tripod is essential. These are large, stable and easy to operate and there is a wide range of accessories such as different heads available.

Angled Viewing Attachment - to look around corners

When using the camera at ground level looking into the viewfinder can be very awkward and focusing and judging the effect difficult. The Nikon Right-Angle Viewing Attachment DR-3, which is attached to the eyepiece of the camera, diverts the light from the viewfinder at a right-angle. This is also useful when used on the copy stand.

The Cameras in Detail

	F	EL	FT2	FM	FE2	FA
Bayonet						
-Nikon F	x	x	x			
-Nikon A1				x	x	
-Nikon A1-S						x
Shutter						
-electrically controlled		x	x	x	x	x
-mechanically controlled	x	1/90			1/250	1/250
-slowest speed (sec)	1	4	1	1	8	1
-fastest speed (sec)	1/1000	1/1000	1/1000	1/1000	1/4000	1/4000
sync speed (sec)	1/60	1/125	1/125	1/125	1/250	1/250
Viewfinder						
-fixed		x	x	x	x	x
-interchangeable	4					
-interchangeable focusing screens	17				3	3
Viewfinder information						
-shutter speed	x*	x	x	x	x	x
-aperture				x	x	x
-overexposure	x*	x	x	x	x	x
-underexposure	x*	x	x	x	x	x
-flash ready					x	x
-flash OK					x	x
Exposure metering						
-selective	x*	x	x	x	x	x
-integral						x
-memory		x			x	
-CdS cell	x*	x	x			
-Ga cell				x		
-Si cell					x	x
Exposure control						
-shutter speed priority						x
-aperture priority		x			x	x
-programmed exposure						x

	F	EL	FT2	FM	FE2	FA
-compensation factors					+/-2	+/-2
Film speeds (ASA values)						
-lowest	6*	25	12	12	12	12
-highest	6400*	1600	1600	3200	4000	4000
Automatic flash						
-automatic setting of sync speed					x	x
-TTL automatic					x	x
Features						
-self timer	x	x	x	x	x	x
-multiple exposure setting				x	x	x
-preview button	x	x	x	x	x	x
-motor drive attachable	x			x	x	x
Dimensions						
-width (mm)	147	145	148	142	142,5	142,5
-height (mm)	103	93,5	96	89,5	90	92
-depth (mm)		54,5	54	60,5	57,5	64,5
-weight (g)	830	780	780	590	550	625

*with Photomic FTN exposure metering finder

Nikon Lens Program 1972-1982

	L	G	NA	SFD	Ft	Wt	72/82
2,8/6 FE	12	9	22	0,25	incl	5200	82
2,8/8 FE	10	8	22	0,3	incl	1000	72
2,8/8 FE	10	8	22	0,3	incl	1100	82
5,6/10 OP FE-X	10	6	22#		incl	400	72
5,6/10 OP FE-X	9	6	22#		incl	400	82
5,6/13	16	12	22	0,3	spec	1200	82
3,5/15	14	11	22	0,3	spec	630	82
2,8/16 FE	8	5	22	0,3	incl	310	82
4/18	13	9	22	0,3	IX	325	82
3,5/20	11	9	22	0,3	72	390	72
3,5/20	11	8	22	0,3	52	235	82
2,8/24	9	7	16	0,3	52	290	72
2,8/24	9	9	22	0,3	52	270	82
2/24	11	10	22	0,3	52	300	82
4/28 PC	10	8	22&	0,3	72	410	82
3,5/28	6	6	16	0,6	52	215	72
3,5/28	6	6	22	0,3	52	235	82
2,8/28	7	7	22	0,3	52	245	82
2,8/28 S.E.	5	5	22	0,3	52	150	82
2/28	9	8	22	0,3	52	345	72
2/28	9	8	22	0,3	52	355	82
2,8/35	7	6	16	0,3	52	200	72
2,8/35	6	6	22	0,3	52	240	82
2,8/35 PC	8	7	32&	0,3	52	335	72
2,8/35 PC	8	7	32&	0,3	52	330	82
2,5/35 S.E.	5	5	22	0,3	52	150	82

	L	G	NA	SFD	Ft	Wt	72/82
2/35	8	6	16	0,3	52	285	72
2/35	8	6	22	0,3	52	280	82
1,4/35	9	7	22	0,3	52	415	72
1,4/35	9	7	16	0,3	52	400	82
2,8/45 GN	4	3	32	0,8	52	155	72
2/50	6	4	16	0,6	52	205	72
1,8/50	6	5	22	0,45	52	220	82
1,8/50 S.E.	6	5	22	0,6	52	135	82
1,4/50	7	5	16	0,6	52	325	72
1,4/50	7	6	16	0,45	52	255	82
1,2/50	7	6	16	0,5	52	390	82
1,2/55	7	5	16	0,6	52	420	72
3,5/55 Micro	5	4	32	0,241	52	235	72
3,5/55 Micro-P	5	4	32	0,241	52	235	72
2,8/55 Micro	6	5	32	0,25	52	240	82
1,2/58 Noct	7	6	16	0,5	52	480	82
2/85	5	5	22	0,85	52	310	82
1,8/85	6	4	22	1,0	52	420	72
2,8/100 S.E.	4	4	22	1	52	255	82
4/105 Micro	5	3	32	0,47	52	500	82
2,5/105	5	4	32	1,0	52	435	72
2,5/105	5	4	22	1,0	52	435	82
3,5/135	4	3	32	1,5	52	470	72
3,5/135	4	4	32	1,3	52	400	82
2,8/135	4	4	22	1,5	52	620	72

L = elements G = Groups NA = narrowest aperture SFD = shortest focusing distance Ft = filter size Wt = weight

	L	G	NA	SFD	Ft	Wt	72/82	
2,8/135	5	4	32	1,3	52	430	82	
2/135	6	4	22	1,3	72	860	82	
2,8/180	5	4	32	1,8	72	830	72	
2,8/180	5	4	32	1,8	72	880	82	
4/200	4	4	32	2	52	630	72	
4/200	5	5	32	2	52	530	82	
4/200 MicroIF	9	6	32	0,71	52	740	82	
5,6/200 MED	4	4	45			670	72	
5,6/200 MED	4	4	45			700	82	
4,5/300	6	5	22	4	72	1060	72	
4,5/300	6	5	22	4	72	1100	82	
4,5/300 IF-ED	7	6	22	2,5	72	990	82	
2,8/300 IF-ED	8	6	22	4	39	2500	82	
5,6/400 IF-ED	7	6	32	4	72	1200	82	
4,5/400+	4	4	22	5	122	1900	72	82
3,5/400 IF-ED	8	6	22	4,5	39	2800	82	
8/500	5	3	8=	4	39	1000	82	
5,6/600+	5	4	22	11	122	2400	72	82
5,6/600 IF-ED	7	6	22	5,5	39	2700	82	
8/800	5	3	8=	4	39	1000	72	
8/800 IF-ED	9	7	32	10	39	3300	82	
8/800+	5	4	22	19	122	2300	72	
8/800+	5	4	64#	19	122	2300	72	
11/1000	5	5	11=	8	34,5	1900	72	
11/1000	5	3	11=	8	39	1900	82	
11/1200+	5	5	64#	43	122	3100	72	
11/1200 IF-ED	9	8	32	14	39	3900	82	
11/2000	5	5	11=	18	incl	17500	82	

	L	G	NA	SFD	Ft	Wt	72/82
4/25-50	11	10	22	0,6	72	600	82
3,5/35-70	10	9	22	1	72	550	82
3,5/43-86	9	7	22	1,2	52	410	72
3,5/43-86	11	8	22	1,2	52	450	82
4,5/50-300	20	13	22	2,5	95	2270	72
4,5/50-300 ED	15	11	32	2,5	95	2200	82
3,5/75-150 S.E.	12	9	32	1	52	520	82
4,5/80-200	15	10	32	1,8	52	830	72
4,5/80-200	12	9	32	1,8	52	750	82
4/85-250	16	9	16	4	IX	1900	72
8/180-600 ED	18	11	32	2,5	95	3400	82
9,5/200-600	19	12	32	4	IX	2300	72
9,5/200-600	19	12	32	4	IX	2400	82
11/360-1200 ED	20	12	32	6	122	7100	82
4/105 BLG	5	3	32&		52	230	72

BLG = lens head which can only be focused with a bellows device
ED = use of ED glass
FE = fisheye
FE-X = fisheye which can only be used with a special finder because the mirror can't be moved due to lens components protruding into the camera body
GN = with X-sync coupling for flash, can also be used normally
IF = internal focusing
MED = medical lens with integral ring flash system
PC = shift lens which can be moved 11mm from the optical axis
S.E. = E series
+ = can only be used with focusing attachment
£ = version with lock iris diaphragm
& = version with pre-selection iris diaphragm
= = mirror lens with fixed iris diaphragm

ACCESSORIES WELL WORTH LOOKING AT!

OP/TECH

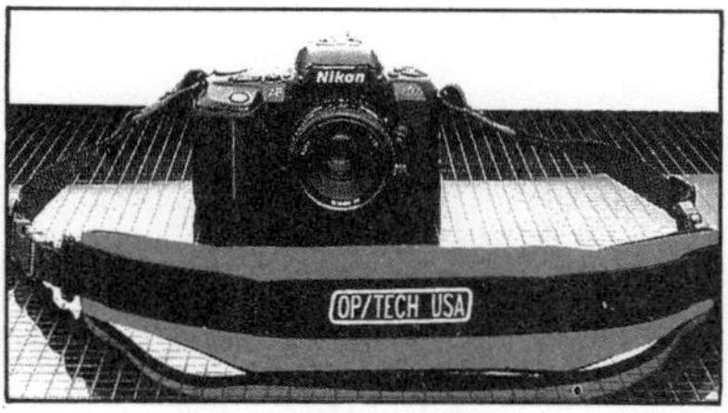

The world's most comfortable cameras, bag and tripod straps (binoculars too). Op/tech has a built-in weight reduction system that makes equipment feel 50% lighter and 100% more comfortable. From the famous 'Pro-Camera Strap' to the 'Bag Strap' and the 'Tripod Strap', the style, colours and comfort which along with the non-slip grip, ensure that you have a wonderful combination of comfort and safety.

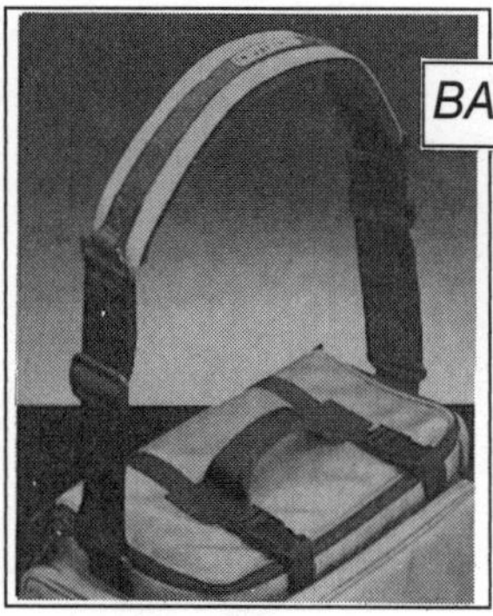

BAG STRAP

The **OP/TECH USA Bag Strap** is the answer to the problem of carrying a heavy bag for extended periods of time. By combining the patented weight reduction system with the Non Slip Grip™, you have the perfect strap for camera/video bags and cases as well as garment bags. Adjustable from 29" to 52", this strap is one of a kind. You will feel the difference!

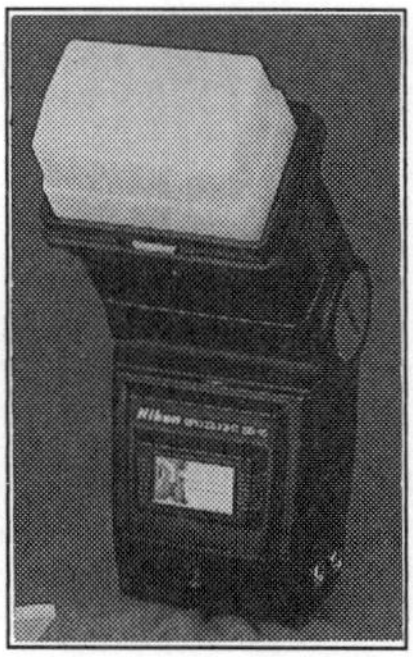

STO-FEN

The ultimate lightweight diffuser system for high powered modern flashguns. Sto-Fen offers the 'Omni-Bounce' for overall soft diffusion – often called the "softie" – which weighs in at just 15 grams and the 'Two-Way' Bounce Card for those who prefer to direct diffused light from their flash. The 'Two-Way' only weighs 25 grams, so it adds almost nothing to the overall weight of the flash. Sto-Fen are the lightest weight, most effective flash diffuser products on the market today.

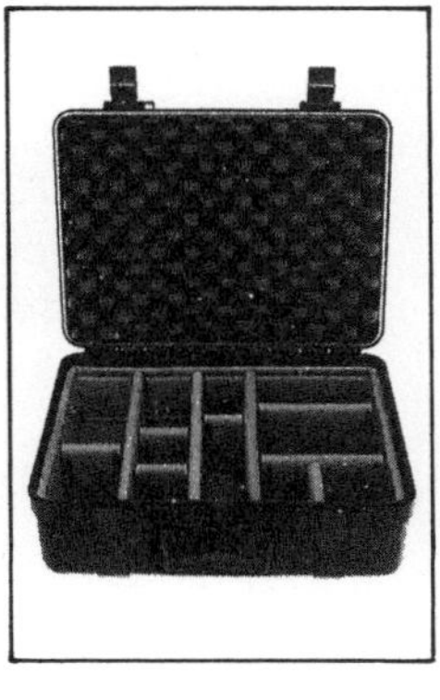

PELI-PELICAN CASES

Watertight and airtight to 30 feet for the ultimate in protection. Constructed of light weight space age structural resin with a neoprene "O" ring seal and exclusive purge valve. Supplied complete with pre-scored pick n'pluck foam or padded dividers. Also includes locking flanges, massive multiple latches for absolute security and best of all, a comfortable molded grip handle.

For a complete list of the many
Hove Foto Books
and User's Guides
for Modern, Classical
and Collectors' Cameras,
write to:-

Worldwide Distribution:

Newpro (UK)
Old Sawmills Road
Faringdon
Oxon
United Kingdom
SN7 7DS
Tel: (01367) 242411
Fax: (01367) 241124

Or from the Publishers:

Hove Foto Books
Jersey Photographic Museum
Hotel de France
St. Saviour's Road
Jersey
Channel Islands
JE2 7LA
Tel: (01534) 614700
Fax: (01534) 887342